The Driftless Land

Spirit of Place in the Upper Mississippi Valley

The Driftless Land

Spirit of Place in the Upper Mississippi Valley

by Kevin Koch

Southeast Missouri State University Press

The Driftless Land: Spirit of Place in the Upper Mississippi Valley
by Kevin Koch

Paper, $19.00
ISBN: 978-0-9822489-6-6

First Published in 2010 in the United States of America by
Southeast Missouri State University Press
MS 2650, One University Plaza
Cape Girardeau, MO 63701
www6.semo.edu/universitypress

Cover design: Liz Lester

Map illustration: Angela Koch

Cover photograph: NPS photo "Sunrise at Firepoint" by Ken Block,
    Chief of Interpretation, Effigy Mounds National Monument

Photography associated with the places described in *The Driftless Land* may be viewed at www.driftlessland.com.

To Dianne,
who has explored these hills and valleys
with me

Acknowledgments and Caveats

The Driftless Land has been nourished by many years of hiking, bicycling, canoeing, cross-country skiing, and snowshoeing in the Upper Mississippi Valley. It has been informed by research, interviews, and guided tours, and capped off with—most importantly—reflection and wonderment. What is it about this place of river bluffs, steep hills, limestone outcroppings, and cascading valleys that so many of us quietly love?

I am indebted to many people who enabled me to write these works. Loras College presented me with the gift of time: a semester's sabbatical to research, write, and hang out in the woods to bring to fruition this work that had been years in the making. Susan Stone, Ph.D., served as Acting Chair of Language and Literature during the semester while I was away. The Loras College Faculty Development Committee awarded me a research grant for travel. The Loras College faculty writing group, The Redactors, offered their insights and suggestions on several of these pieces.

Loras Psychology Professor cum musician Bob Dunn deserves my gratitude for his inspiration in collaborating with me on a companion multi-media program titled "The Driftless Land." He, along with fellow musician Louis Fautsch, added music and photography to these meager words, all in celebration of this rugged landscape.

My wife Dianne deserves many thanks. She has ventured out to most of these places with me, listened to my ramblings as I pondered each work, offered feedback, and put up with my time away from home when travels took me elsewhere.

My children—Paul, Brian, and Angie—are no longer at those childhood ages when it was easy for all of us to head out to the woods together, but they too have put up with the many hours I've been sequestered at the computer and have stoically endured my enthusiasm about the places I describe here.

Finally, I wish to thank the many people who have granted me interviews and responded to my email correspondences and phone calls, and who have allowed me to tag along with them through the woods and on the river. I am infinitely richer for having met each and every one of you.

I have tried to be as accurate as possible in researching the geology, history, and stories of the places I have visited in the Driftless Land. I apologize in advance for any errors that undoubtedly have crept into the text. The textual, electronic, and personal interview resources are acknowledged in a separate section at the end of the book.

If it is possible to thank the land itself, I would like to do so. There is a spirit of place in the Driftless Land, and that Spirit has allowed me occasional glimpses of things deeper than bedrock. For that I am forever grateful.

Previous publications:

"Savanna Army Depot," "Manitoumie. Sinisinawa." and "The Rivers That Bring Us Together" appeared in *Big Muddy: A Journal of the Mississippi River Valley*.

Portions of "Hiking the Driftless," and "Whitewater-Lost Canyon" appeared as shorter pieces in the *Dubuque Telegraph Herald Tri-State Outdoors Magazine*.

Table of Contents

THE DRIFTLESS LAND

To speak of this ground as a mystery is not to say that we know nothing, only that we cannot know everything.

—Scott Russell Sanders, "Ground Notes,"
Staying Put: Making a Home in a Restless World

READING THE EARTH

how letters scratched and etched
across a page
suggest a sound,
whole words,
how meaning rises up like a mist
where there is just ink
on a flat landscape

how the plains speak
of the scraping glaciers,
limestone moans
of ancient seas,
how river bluffs
are carved slates
and meaning, like a mist,
rises up from fissures in the rock

how with time
and a little tutelage
we learn
to read the earth.

The Driftless Land

> *General to particular. Everything had a*
> *name. To live fully in a place all your life*
> *you kept aiming smaller and smaller in*
> *attention to detail.*
> —Charles Frazier, *Cold Mountain*

Driftless.

My thoughts are poised this day on an overlook of the Mississippi, four hundred feet above the mile-wide expanse of river, taking in the view of the forested bluffs hugging the shorelines and a small town basking in the floodplain. Just as quickly I am inland, in a deep ravine of tumbled limestone boulders and fragile broken shale, where a small stream erupts from a spring and the damp chill guards against the summer's oppressive heat. I am on a rounded hill in winter, at the edge of woods, cross-country skiing as daylight fades, my body warm against the icy wind.

I am pedaling up a steep incline at the Mines of Spain, luxuriating in the fullness of summer sweat. I am hiking with my wife on a trail that climbs—and drops and climbs again—from stream bottom to river bluff, through woods and fingerling prairies. I have stumbled onto a Native American burial mound hidden in the woods, silent, forgotten, unnoticeable except for a slight swell against the lay of the land. In my backyard I nurture a late-night campfire, or admire the clean line the snow blower has cut along the driveway against the soft and otherwise unbroken snowfall at dawn.

My thoughts put me anywhere, everywhere, in the places that I know in the Driftless Land. It is what I have sometimes imagined the afterlife to be, a movement of soul like the wind across the landscape.

Driftless.

———————

A driftless person is aimless, a wanderer. While I may occasionally set my thoughts adrift, I'm too Midwestern to be truly without a compass. To the contrary, I am rooted in family, professions of work and of spirit, and—increasingly—to the ground I walk on—the Driftless Land.

Outsiders know the Midwest as flatlands, as oceans of corn pressing toward the horizon beneath a big sky. Lesser known are the steep hills and bluffs, the ravines and towering rock outcroppings where the Mississippi River carves its meandering path. These rugged lands amid the prairies are known as the Driftless Area, a 20,000 square-mile region of northeast Iowa, northwest Illinois, southeast Minnesota, and southwest and central Wisconsin bypassed by most of the glaciers, the last ones ending some twelve thousand years ago, just yesterday in geologic time.

I like to imagine the edge of ice. Here, on somebody's farm, the glacier would have limped to a halt, checked by a reverse in climate. Behind it lay half a continent of ice, up to two miles thick, the land pressed and ground flat beneath it. Beyond the glacier's edge, the hilly land lay beneath a thick snow, spared the bulldozing and grinding of the relentless ice. This land, already hilly, would be further eroded for centuries by meltwater when the warming began, resulting in great bluffs rising mightily from the Mississippi and steep, rounded fingers of woodland sharply etched by tumbling ravines.

Geologists aren't completely sure why the glaciers ignored this sliver of land. Some speculate that the hard igneous uplands of north-central Wisconsin may have diverted or slowed the advancing ice. The glaciers slid over the uplands, but lost their momentum before reaching the Driftless Land.

But geologists are storytellers, never fully certain of the past. They gather evidence and piece together the puzzle as best they can.

We're all storytellers, set down in a particular place and time, trying to make sense of it all. Here in the Driftless Land, the Mississippi tells a story of endless movement, of time's onward march and the everchanging fluidity of life. In contrast, the bluffs and rock outcroppings—the protruding tips of the solid bone of earth—give us grounding.

Impermanence and solidity. The very continents drift on a subterranean sea of magma, thrusting up mountains when they collide, opening up the sea floor to lava eruptions when they slide apart. On the other hand, what happens on earth stays on earth. With the exception perhaps of some stray molecules at the earth's high atmosphere and some NASA spacecraft blasted into outer space, matter from the earth's creation is still with us, along with the material stuff of our ancestors, which, if not recycled into new plant and animal life, is embedded in the soil and whirling through the universe right along with the rest of us.

Impermanence and solidity are linked in sacred bond. The land itself is sacred. Certain places call to their inhabiting peoples. Celtic tradition calls them the "thin" places, where only a gossamer veil divides the earthen world from the spirits. But all places have stories—how they were formed by mountain or sea, crushed or spared by glacier, when they encountered the first human, if at all—and story is what gives the land its spirit, breath, and sacramental nature.

There is story here in the Driftless Land, in its river bluffs and limestone towers, in its recovering woods and prairies, and in the successive waves of humanity who have washed over it. The Driftless Land is thick with story and thus—paradoxically—one of the thin places. On a misty morning on the road to Galena you can almost see through to the other side.

———————————

The Driftless Land—more frequently but less poetically called the Driftless Area by mapmakers—is said to begin around Fort Snelling at the confluence of the Minnesota and Mississippi Rivers just southeast of Minneapolis. On its western boundary, it ventures only a few miles beyond the Mississippi. Its Minnesota, Wisconsin, Iowa, and Illinois river towns include Trempeleau, Winona, La Crosse, McGregor, Prairie du Chien, Guttenberg, Dubuque, Bellevue, and Savanna. It peters out along the Mississippi several miles south of the Mississippi Palisades (Illinois) State Park where it makes an impressive last stand with 300-foot sheer-bluff river overlooks. To the east, the Driftless Land broadens into the hills and rock outcroppings of west-central Wisconsin, and counts among its towns Eau Claire, Tomah, Spring Green, Dodgeville, and Mineral Point. In Illinois its easternmost push is to Galena, a historic lead mining town of bluffs and brick.

The term itself—"Driftless"—means that there is little or no glacial drift in these regions. No drumlins or eskers laid down by streams and meltwater-holes in the glacier, no glacial erratics (rounded boulders left indiscriminately behind in glacially scraped flatlands), no hilly moraines piled up where the glacier ended its trek down the continent, no wind-blown loess sculpted into ridge-topped hills. The glaciers re-sculpted most of the upper half of North America. The Driftless Land offers a glimpse of the Midwest before the arrival of the icy beast: limestone and sandstone bluffs and towers, crumbling shale, sharp ravines, rolling hills, caves, river overlooks.

But geologists are spoilsports, and in the end it seems that the name may turn out to be a misnomer, especially when loosely applied. If by "driftless" you mean only that it escaped the last great glaciers of the Wisconsinan period just a scant twelve thousand years ago, that is true, but so did all but about one-third of Iowa and Illinois, including lands well beyond the so-called "Driftless," although these other regions still sport a generous topping of drift from earlier glacial periods. On the other hand, if by "driftless" you mean that it escaped *all* glacial periods dating back 2.5 million years, then more recent evidence suggests that the true Driftless may be significantly smaller, limited to west-central Wisconsin and a slight wedge of northwest Illinois. Geologists prefer the term "Paleozoic Plateau" to indicate the ancient sedimentary rock structures that underlie this uniquely rugged terrain. Suffice it to say that parts of the Driftless

may have seen the most ancient of glaciers. But the evidence
is mostly worn away.

Spoilsports perhaps, but geologists aren't poets. Don't expect
"Paleozoic Plateau" to replace "the Driftless Land" on anyone's tongue
just yet. We need metaphor to sustain the spirits of the land, and
"Driftless" hints at something behind and beneath the rocks. "Driftless" carries morning mists and the weight of memory in the thin
places more than "Paleozoic" will ever do.

So, Driftless it will be.

I was surprised to learn that there is indeed a Driftless Area
National Wildlife Refuge. It's tiny by comparison to its companion
places in the national refuge system. Administered from the same
McGregor office that oversees a district of the Upper Mississippi
National Fish and Wildlife Refuge (which covers 240,000 acres from
Minnesota to southern Iowa), the Driftless refuge protects a mere 781
acres scattered across nine sites in northeast Iowa. The smallest site is
a scant six acres.

All but one of the sites are closed to the public, partly because
some are sequestered within folds of private property and partly because they protect incredibly fragile ecosystems. Typically, the Driftless Refuge sites offer tiny windows to the immediate post-glacial
past. Sinkholes and steep hillside vents in the limestone outcroppings
create micro-environments reminiscent of a cooler climate. The chilly
air pockets harbor threatened and endangered plants and animals
like the Northern Monkshood flower and the Iowa Pleistocene snail.

In April, I hiked the one public area, the Howard Creek Unit, the
largest tract at 209 acres, located in Clayton County. Howard Creek
was a new find for me, but it felt familiar with its steep-cliffed overlooks of the valley floor. Deer and wild turkeys blossomed from thin
air in the forest as I descended to the creek. Recent snowmelt made
the creek impassable unless I wanted to wade into waters up to my
hips, but I could still get close enough to the table-sized limestone
blocks that littered the rapids after having long ago been sloughed

off from the creek-edged bluff. For a while I pulled up a grassy seat alongside a small U-shaped waterfall and watched a spring unload fresh water from the side of a rock. When I climbed back out of the valley, I sidestepped mole hills and chose my path through patches of winter-browned tallgrass prairie that had been flattened by deer.

Tiny refuge plots, hidden from the public view, issuing forth cool micro-climates from vents in the bedrock and offering a glimpse to the past. It was all very appropriate to the Driftless Land, relatively unknown and undiscovered in a pocket within the glacially sculpted Midwest.

It had all the markings of the thin places.

———————————

I admire those who, unlike myself, can disentangle bird calls into Henslowe sparrow and scarlet tanager. I admire those who, after a quick glance at a rock outcropping, can tell you whether it is Silurian or Ordovician limestone. They know the world they inhabit down to its specifics.

Place is like that. You can "love nature" and "love the land," but you won't know place until you've walked slowly and attentively through Lost Canyon or the Kickapoo Valley Reserve or Swiss Valley or Trempealeau Mountain, and then returned to learn what you can about them. Even that is abstraction, too broad for a sense of place, for within Lost Canyon is a four-foot wide ice cave that in winter gives birth to ice figures that seem spookily alive. At Swiss Valley a burr oak hides in the furthermost trail where the Catfish Creek floodplain meets a hillside swell. You ski past its brown bones in February, and in July its thick foliage offers cool relief to the sweat on your brow. A sense of place requires that you know where the small, century-old lead-mine pits are in the valley preserve near your house, and know where the wild turkeys congregate on the hilltop clearing.

But place is not without people. Indeed, perhaps people are a requirement for place. Mars has a land surface, but it takes people to add the drop of magic that brings meaning to land and creates a sense of place. Here in the Driftless, the first humans wandered at the edge of the glaciers twelve thousand years ago, hunting mastodons and other megafauna. The story isn't clear—perhaps never will be—but perhaps their ancestors or other wandering tribes became the Hopewellian peoples who built burial and ceremonial mounds in the shape of birds and bears on the Mississippi bluffs. A few more ticks of the clock and other migrations brought the Mesquakie to my neck of the woods, and the Sauk and Ho-Chunk and the Kickapoo to other areas of the Driftless. Tragedy and genocide played out as European-Americans arrived, but as the bloodshed began to be conveniently forgotten, the next to settle were simple farmers, lead-miners, and those eager to set up shops in fledgling towns.

Meaning arises from the interaction of people and place. I have never visited the far reaches of the Boy Scout Trail at the Mines of Spain with anyone but my wife, Dianne. The meaning of place, in that instance, for me, is entwined with the meaning of her. Other times, my most memorable walks throughout the Driftless have included other friends and wildlife guides. In that sense, the precise meaning of place will be different for everyone.

But sometimes solitude and silence are the best companions when you want to find meaning welling up like vapor from the fissures in the rock. Snowshoeing alone in late winter, I have weaved into thick woods and marveled at the quiet cold. In late-night cross-country ventures on the golf course near my home, I've paused at the lip of the steepest hill and watched the moon, the forest edge, and burr oak shadows. I am more likely to notice the season's first wave of warm sun and the sudden cooling of a breeze, if I am not distracted by conversation. The crunch and swish of maple leaves in the October woods is most intense when I am by myself.

There is meaning in the land, in the sacred places, but they are meanings only sensed, not known. In the Driftless Land, the limestone bluffs keep a stony silence, the hills and valleys keep their stories buried. Deep within the bedrock may lie a fossil never seen. Beneath a forest soil there may be ancient burial mounds. A rusted piece of iron in the woods may be left over from lead-miners or early pioneers.

Listening quietly in the woods will not loosen the stories from the land. But listening takes me deep within myself to a place where the Driftless Land itself is sacred.

The Rivers That Bring
Us Together

We are hiking past the marching bears.

The Mississippi River slips quietly downstream beneath the bluff to our left. The woods are thick at our right, barren and brown in early December. Alongside us lie the Native American burial mounds of the Effigy Mounds National Monument near the town of Marquette in northeast Iowa. Conical mounds, linear mounds, and effigies in the shapes of flying birds and great marching bears point downstream.

Just south of here the Wisconsin River empties into the Mississippi, a confluence of waters that brought native tribes together at this sacred spot, brought the European trader, and even brought them together in a frontier village of interracial marriage, until, in the end, it all came tumbling down.

Above it all the ancient burial mounds—hundreds of them— silent in the progression of seasons. The marching bears keep pointing downstream.

Winter is holding off this year. Dennis Lenzendorf, a Prairie du Chien, Wisconsin, science teacher and seasonal park ranger and guide at Effigy Mounds, bounces us up the rocky service road in his Jeep, taking us high into the hills of the park's secluded South Unit, taking us to the marching bears. On December 4 it is 45 degrees, and you can bet that the mild weather won't last.

He knows the story like it is written in his bones.

Effigy Mounds National Monument—established in 1949—pre-serves and protects over two hundred burial and ceremonial mounds—thirty-one of them in the shapes of bears or birds—in one of the nation's most significant Native American historical and spiri-tual sites. The mounds range from 750 to 2,500 years old, the work of Woodland Period Native Americans, a hunter-gatherer society that inhabited the Mississippi River valley and bluffs and the oak savanna prairies that stretched over the inland rolling hills.

The Mississippi and Wisconsin Rivers were great highways—stretching north to Minnesota and northeast nearly to the Great Lakes and south as far as the imagination could reach. The rivers gathered the Woodland Period clans together each spring at the junc-tion. There they fished the rivers, tended gardens, hunted, and set up trading posts.

In late fall, the clans dispersed far and near—small bands and families—in search of rock shelters in which to endure the winter, each group to its own devices. In spring the rivers brought them to-gether again in celebration.

They brought the winter's dead—interred over-winter in tree platforms—to the gathering place, and the season's work of mound building began. First, the builders scored the mound's shape into the blufftop soil, although some of the mounds are at river flood-plain level. The dead were interred in the scored-out basins of the mounds. Next, the Woodland peoples carried soil, basket by basket, from the sacred river bank up winding paths to the top of the 450-foot bluff, and spread it layer after layer upon the mounds, interspersed with clam shells, ornaments, weapons, and other cremated ashes. Slowly they raised the mounds to a height of four to five feet above the savanna floor.

Most mounds, and the oldest, are conical or linear. Conical mounds are usually ten to twenty feet in diameter. Linear mounds are typically six to eight feet wide and stretch thirty or fifty feet in length. One linear mound in the park is 470 feet long.

But it is the effigy mounds that define this place, and as we exit his

Jeep and begin our hike, Dennis points to the large bear and
bird images along the path. These later-period mounds were built
from 500 through 1250 AD. The largest bear lumbers 137 feet from
nose to tail and the largest bird spreads its wings 212 feet. Some effigies were burial mounds, but many were ceremonial. Ash residue
pinpoints the ceremonial fire pit, often located at the heart of the bear
or bird. Great ceremonies amid the bear and bird effigies linked land
and sky, human and earth, spirit and beast. Rituals celebrated the
harvest, prepared the peoples for winter, and rejoiced in the renewal
of spring. These ceremonies, says Dennis, actively involved the tribe
in bringing forth the new season, a sacred responsibility of the peoples along the river.

There may have been Keepers of the Mounds, Dennis says, spiritual landscapers of sorts, who kept watch over this magnificent overlook of the Mississippi from the oak savanna that graced the blufftop.

Today the Park Service is Keeper of the Mounds. In a moment
of skepticism, I ask Dennis whether Native Americans resent the
mounds being put on public display. He considers the question
thoughtfully, but shakes his head, no: "A tribal elder from Wisconsin has said that if the Park Service weren't here, there would be no
mounds preserved. And we not only preserve the mounds, but also
the landscape that goes with them. Tribal peoples say that we are
preserving a sacred space, a sacred geography."

Indeed, Dennis draws my attention equally to the woods, the
river, and the mounds themselves. On an earlier visit, I had climbed
the trail that rises some 450 feet above the interpretive center on
the valley floor to the blufftop. Markers along the switch-back trail
announced the rich variety of the forest: walnut, basswood, sugar
maple, white oak, red cedar, white ash, chinkapin oak, shagbark
hickory, hawthorn, honey locust, black cherry, big-toothed aspen, red
oak.

"There's a meaning here that is many layers deep," Dennis says,
insisting that the land, forest, prairie, river, and burial mounds are
all part of a seamless web. "The Native Americans understood that.
We're getting closer."

Later, as we descend the rocky service road to a fading December sun, Dennis wraps up his thoughts. The mound-building ended about 750 years ago, he says. The Woodland Period peoples spread out across the prairie. Their descendents became the Oneota, later the Ioway, perhaps even the Sioux and the Ho-Chunk. They moved away. But their spiritual connection with the land did not die away. "According to tribal historians," he says, "many practices observed today have their roots in the Effigy Mound Culture."

Other tribes like the Mesquakie and the Sauk, driven out of the eastern woodlands by the Iroquois, took their place along the river bluffs, arriving in the early 1700s. Settling first in Wisconsin, they came down the Wisconsin River to settle along the Mississippi, at the base of the mounds, and up and down the Iowa, Wisconsin, and Illinois shores.

The rivers brought them here.

I once came upon Native American burial mounds in a most inauspicious way. In a snowless winter, in the woods above the Mississippi near my home in Dubuque, Iowa, I spied in the distance what I first took to be a long-abandoned pioneer lead-mine pit, a circular indentation in the ground too neatly round to be a sinkhole. I pushed through the brush beyond the trail in order to check it out. As I drew nearer, though, I realized it did not have the tell-tale signs of a lead-mine pit. It wasn't deep and cone-shaped. There was no ring of rock at its lip, no boulders dug up and dropped at the pit's edge. I looked around in the woods for similar small craters, since lead-mine pits often occur in linear groups, frequently in east-west runs where miners had caught a line of lead along a limestone fracture.

I looked east, I looked west. Two more circles dotted the nearby soil, but these were not pits but mounds rising up from the forest floor. Native American burial mounds? But what about the pit? Maybe it *was* just a lead-mine remnant, but more likely—given the location among the other mounds—it was some long-ago desecration of the grave by a fool with a shovel. I had no way of knowing. My skin crawled, and I hurried back to the trail.

From the trail I could see the Mississippi River through winter's denuded branches and tree trunks, as silent as it was when the Woodland peoples buried their dead on the blufftops.

The European arrival on the upper Mississippi River was, at first, a drop here, a drop there. Father Jacques Marquette and explorer Louis Joliet arrived first, by canoe, in 1673. From his mission church along Lake Michigan, Marquette was summoned by the French governor to accompany Joliet to find a passageway to the Far East.

Marquette and Joliet had heard of a great river that bisected the continent, heading south to the oceans. How could they reach it from the Great Lakes? The Miami of the Green Bay area agreed to show them the route. They would paddle up the Fox River that fed into the Great Lakes and then portage several miles to the Wisconsin River, which flowed southwest to the Mississippi, the Father of Waters.

Marquette kept a journal: "The River on which we embarked is called Meskousing [Wisconsin]. It is very wide; it has a sandy bottom, which forms various shoals that render its navigation very difficult. It is full of Islands."

Marquette, Joliet, and their men paddled southwest, past woods, prairies, and bluffs. They passed an iron mine worked by the Native Americans. Soon the Wisconsin began to widen and deepen: "We arrived at the mouth of our River; and, at 42 and half degrees Of latitude, We safely entered the Mississippi on the 17th of June, with a Joy that I cannot Express."

From Pike's Peak State Park on the Iowa bluff, 450 feet above the river across from the confluence of the Wisconsin and Mississippi, you will see what Marquette next describes:

Here we are, then, on this so renowned River. . . . It is narrow at the place where Miskous [Wisconsin] empties; its Current, which flows southward, is slow and gentle. To the right is a large Chain of very high Mountains, and to the left are beautiful lands; in various Places, the stream is Divided by Islands.

Marquette describes the fish and wildlife encountered there, perhaps with an exaggerated or fear-induced flair:

> From time to time, we came upon monstrous fish, one of which struck our Canoe with such violence that I Thought that it was a great tree, about to break the Canoe to pieces. On another occasion, we saw on the water a monster with the head of a tiger, a sharp nose Like That of a wildcat, with whiskers and straight, Erect ears; the head was grey and The Neck quite black.

And finally he spies the "wild cattle":

> They are very similar to our domestic cattle. They are not longer, but are nearly as large again, and more Corpulent. When Our people killed one, three persons had much difficulty in moving it. The head is very large; The forehead is flat, and a foot and a half Wide between the Horns, which are exactly like Those of our oxen, but black and much larger. Under the Neck They have a Sort of large dewlap, which hangs down; and on The back is a rather high hump. The whole of the head, The Neck, and a portion of the Shoulders, are Covered with a thick Mane Like That of horses.

Jacques Marquette had, of course, just experienced his first sighting of the American bison.

Marquette and Joliet would paddle as far south as present day Arkansas, where a budding fear of the Native Americans and the Spaniards to the south turned them back.

On both passages, south and north, they had slipped beneath and alongside the ancient effigy burial mounds, without ever knowing they were there. They had arrived and returned via the junction of the Mississippi and Wisconsin Rivers, just like so many before them.

We enjoy our rivers, have made them into our playthings. The

Wisconsin River is a canoeist's delight, with its swift current, sandy bottom and ample sand islands, and comparatively clean waters—you can see your paddle two feet down, as compared to most Midwest rivers and streams that are choked, chocolate brown, with eroded mud and thick with fertilizer-induced algae.

I used to canoe the Wisconsin with the Boy Scouts when my sons were younger. We played keep-away by teams while floating down-river, tossing a football from canoe to canoe, working our hardest to overturn the other guys. We played Gooberball on the islands—softball with a duct-tape ball and a canoe paddle for a bat. I declined the game of tackle football. There were other ways to abuse my forty-ish body than to be slammed into the sand by high-strung teenagers.

Now I return from time to time with friends and family. Today my wife and I have taken our two canoes (Rocky and Bullwinkle) and four of our friends on a nine-mile Labor Day float. Dirk and Lorilee alternately laugh uncontrollably or debate a finer point about Thoreau. Since Dinesh and Stephanie are expecting a baby, Steph gets to ride like Cleopatra, although being stuffed into the belly of a canoe bottom hardly makes for a glorious passage.

It's been a dry fall, and we occasionally drag the canoes over low spots in the river. We eat our lunch on a sandy island. Only I am foolish enough to take repeated float trips in my life jacket in the chilling water as we rest.

We draw nearer to our take-out, and the current deepens and quickens. We hug the left shore to avoid the shallow sand shoals, and the current begins to sweep us along. Too late from the rear of the canoe I spot a log protruding from the water, and the current is pushing us toward it! A quick maneuver fails and the canoe capsizes, spilling Lorilee, Dinesh, and me, laughing and yelling and joking. Lorilee catches the log and hangs on for dear life, until we convince her that she can put her feet down and stand up. But the cooler is floating downstream, the handle loosened from the upset. The beer is loose! *My apple is gone*! shouts Dinesh, laughing at the absurdity of it all.

My reputation has floated away, too. So this is the experienced canoeist, they joke for the rest of the trip. When the other canoe returns, having rounded a bend and not seen us for a while, we are

back in the canoe and delirious with laughter. The other canoe catches the one paddle we have not been able to retrieve.

Such is a day on the Wisconsin River, some miles above the
Mississippi, well out of sight of the Effigy Mounds, unless, of course,
some unnamed mounds lurk in the bluffs above us, with only a beating sun and a rustling breeze to suggest the other world.

The bluff at Pikes Peak State Park on the Iowa shore rises 500
feet above the Mississippi, directly across from the confluence of the
Wisconsin River. The view is expansive, stretching upriver to the
town of Prairie du Chien, Wisconsin, lying sleepily in the river floodplain, downriver to Pool #10, river waters backed up by the Lock &
Dam at Guttenberg, Iowa, and directly across to where the Wisconsin
River bleeds into the Mississippi. Together their waters wind and curl
among a hundred islands, and fishing boats anchor in the myriad
cuts in hopes of landing bass and walleye. At eye level across the
river, the rolling hills of Wisconsin bound away on the plateau above
the river valley.

Raging meltwaters scoured the deep river valley as the last glaciers retreated twelve thousand years ago, just yesterday in geologic
time. These rugged bluffs of the Driftless Land escaped the final
glaciers that bulldozed and pulverized everything in their paths. Even
so, the Driftless Land was sculpted by the meltwater, and the Mississippi ran brim to brim across the 400-foot bluffs, and probably even
deeper, since the river floor here contains another 300 feet of glacial
sediment before hitting bedrock.

The down-cutting unveiled a geological past, deep and silent in
the exposed bluff along Pikes Peak State Park. From top to bottom,
the bluff tells a story:

- Galena limestone, formed in deep, quiet seas 450 million
  years ago, with few fossils;
- Decorah limestone and shale, formed in a shallow sea near
  shore, laced with brachiopod fossils;
- Platteville limestone, an impervious layer from which water
  seeps today in outcroppings and forms small waterfalls;

- St. Peter Sandstone, formed from a sandy beach;
- Prairie du Chien Group, layers of dolomite, sandstone, and shale;
- Jordan sandstone, the oldest rock visible at river level, 550 million years old.

Between epochs, the land sometimes heaved upward, rolling back the seas, and sank again, falling beneath new oceans with new, strange creatures dropping into the muck upon their deaths. One last time the land heaved upward, its sea beds now hardened into rock, then bowed beneath or miraculously escaped successive waves of glaciers and were eroded again by their meltwaters raging down the Mississippi and its tributaries.

Pikes Peak State Park takes its name from General Zebulon Pike, whose name likewise graces the more famous Pikes Peak of the Colorado Rocky Mountains. Shortly after the Louisiana Purchase, General Pike paddled up the Mississippi on a mission to scout a likely location for a military fort, and recommended the blufftop with its expansive view. The U.S. government, however, eventually decided on a location just to the north at Prairie du Chien, at river level.

Because the river brings us and gathers us and disperses us.

The town of Prairie du Chien, Wisconsin (population 6,000), lies along the Mississippi River about five miles above the Wisconsin River confluence. Today its major businesses include a 3M Company plant and a Cabela's fishing, hunting, and camping store and warehouse. Named as the Prairie of the Dogs, the town's history is richly intertwined with the Mississippi and nearby Wisconsin rivers, Native American trade and tribal councils, French miners and traders, and military outposts and treaties.

Not far upstream from Effigy Mounds, where ancient tribes rendezvoused from spring through autumn, Prairie du Chien was first a Mesquakie village, a center for trade among tribes and later with the Europeans, and a frequent site of intertribal councils. When the British explorer Jonathan Carver saw the Native American village in

1766, he described it as "one of the most delightsome settlements I saw during my travels," and Peter Pond, a trader from New England, described the village's bustling activity in his 1773 journal:

> We Saw a Large Collection from Everey Part of the Misseppey who had arrived Beforur Us Even from Orleans Eight Hundred Leages Beloue us . . . Hear was Sport of All Sorts we went to Colecting furs and Skins . . . . Thare was Not Les then One Hundred and thirtey Canues.

French fur traders and lead-miners who had arrived shortly after Marquette and Joliet soon settled down and intermarried with the Native Americans, making Prairie du Chien a frontier interracial, Métis village. According to Dr. Thomas Auge, former professor of History at Loras College, by 1781 a number of French traders had purchased land, settled down, built homes, and took Native American wives. The village had grown to 37 houses and nearly 400 people by the time General Pike visited in 1805. Pike, not nearly as accepting of the interracial marriages as the French, wrote with an edge that "almost on half of the inhabitants under 20 years have the blood of the aborigine in their vein." But Pike had to admit that the Métis lived a good life: "the inside furniture of their homes is decent, and indeed, in those of the most wealthy display a degree of elegance and taste."

The Métis culture flourished in Prairie du Chien along with numerous other such villages along the upper Mississippi and Great Lakes, acceptable to Frenchmen and Mesquakie alike, but less so to the American pioneers, miners, and businessmen who began arriving at the village with more frequency by the 1820s. Caleb Atwater wrote with disdain of "as motely a group of creatures, (I can scarcely call them human beings) as the world ever beheld." Their mixed breeding, he denounced, was probably "touched by the Prairie wolf" and had resulted in the vices and faults of each culture "without even one redeeming feature."

The river was soon to disperse them.

Everything begins to unravel.

The Americans build Fort Shelby on the islands near Prairie du Chien in 1814. The British capture the fort, occupy it for several months, and then destroy it. The Americans rebuild it as Fort Crawford in 1816. Sauk and Mesquakie from the river shores to the south meet with Sioux from the north at the white man's fort and draw a line to separate their warring tribes. Soon the military focus shifts from separating warring tribes to securing land for white men, as miners and farmers move illegally onto Native American soil. Tensions flare. Ambushes and revenge. Tribe against tribe, pioneer and soldier against Indian. The U.S. Government forces eight million acres to be ceded for mining interests. The Mississippi River becomes the defacto western boundary for pioneers, and even that is porous.

The Sauk and their cousins the Mesquakie fight back in the Black Hawk War of 1832, attempting to resettle their former lands. For a while, Black Hawk wins, handing defeat to the Illinois militia (including the young officer, Abraham Lincoln) as the Sauk cross the Mississippi and push north through Illinois and southern Wisconsin.

But soon the war turns sour for Black Hawk, ending in massacre about forty miles north of Prairie du Chien in early August when American troops on foot and gunners on the boat "The Warrior" open fire on the remnants of Black Hawk's renegade band of braves, women, and children as they attempt to flee westward across the Mississippi River. Sioux warriors—invited down from the north to join in the melee—finish off most of the rest on the river's western shore. Black Hawk himself surrenders at Fort Crawford in late August.

The time it takes the river to wash the blood downstream pales alongside the river's deep memory.

By then, the spirits entombed in the Effigy Mounds had already been asleep for centuries.

————————————

I see the Mississippi almost every day. In summer I canoe its backwaters. In winter, I go to spot bald eagles. My office window sports a distant view of the river from five stories up on a bluff.

We all share this river. It hosts our picnics, and we boat on it and float barges on it. Sometimes it drowns our children, and sometimes it floods our towns.

It is what it is, and communicates nothing and feels nothing. This is not out of insolence. The river was here first and is not required to be on our terms.

I have neglected to tell you this. At the Effigy Mounds, Dennis Lenzendorf parks the Jeep at the side of the service road along a blufftop prairie. "Come," he says, "I'll show you a rock shelter where we have archaeological evidence of Native Americans over-wintering."

Dennis leads me down through the prairie that is browning out with the lateness of the season. We pick our way through a small woods and turn a sharp corner onto a narrow ledge that overlooks a deep, wooded ravine that has arisen seemingly out of nowhere. Soon the path opens into an indentation in the rock, a shelter perhaps thirty feet long, ten wide, with a ceiling seven feet tall at the opening—though sloping quickly down to nothing at the interior wall.

"Evidence of two-thousand-year-old pottery and campfires have been discovered here," Dennis says, explaining that the tribes that gathered at the Effigy Mounds for the spring, summer, and fall would have dispersed by families or small groups of kinsmen throughout the region to spend the winter before regrouping again in spring. A family would winter along this ravine, hunting deer and rabbits, rationing out corn, and stringing blankets or hides across the rock shelter's entrance to keep out the cold during nights and periods of bad weather.

Two weeks later the mild weather has ended. Back at my home about an hour south of Effigy Mounds, the first winter snowfall is blustering in.

And from the warmth of my house, I can't shake the image: an ancient Indian family packing along the narrow ledge—children afoot, perhaps aiding an elderly grandmother—setting up a winter camp at the rock shelter and starting a fire behind the new-strung hides. And an Indian man, perhaps my age, watching the woods fill up with first snow. How long it will seem until spring.

And when spring comes, the rivers will reunite us here at the confluence of the Wisconsin and Mississippi. We will spend the summer together, raise our crops, hunt, enjoy life. And bury our dead.

But for now it is still winter. The cold is harsh.

Is it warmer now, is it an easier life, with one's bones interred in the mounds and one's spirit free above the rivers?

Winter Here

Now the lone world is streaky as a wall of marble/With veins of clear and frozen snow.
—Thomas Merton, "Evening: Zero Weather," from *Figures for an Apocalypse*

The people I work with know well enough not to be around me when it snows. I am the kid in the office, antsy, gleeful, checking to see whether enough has accumulated for cross-country skiing. "We're happy you're happy," they say, with little enthusiasm.

This winter they've begun to say, "Enough already, Kevin!"

The average snowfall for Dubuque, Iowa, is 43.6 inches per year. Not nearly enough, in my opinion, and in recent years we've rarely hit the average, due to warmer winters. This year, however, we've reached our snow goal and then some. With 80 inches, we've crushed the previous record.

Enough already! But let's see if we can break it again next year.

———————————

This winter has brought me several times to Swiss Valley for cross-country skiing. Swiss Valley is a five-hundred-acre county nature-preserve on Dubuque's west side, named for the Swiss settlers who homesteaded there in 1833. It is a favorite hiking area for my wife and me, and a cross-country skiing haven in winter. Shale out-croppings spill forth cold springs and marshes on the hillsides, a clear, stocked, trout stream slices through the valley, vertical cave openings on the hillside puff snowflakes into the air in winter, and on the dry top ridges the cedars wring a dusty subsistence out of the thin soil atop the limestone.

Today, a fresh six inches of snow has turned small stones in the creek into soft-edged, white islands and has heaped round balls like hydrangeas in the underbrush. But it is warming slightly when we set out, and on one hillside the heavy snow has begun to droop from the twiggy branches, like garland.

The ski-groomer has etched a fresh, packed trail, making the glide easy along the creek, a quick and fluid skimming across the valley. At the far end of the trail, where park property abuts the monastery woods, a swinging bridge crosses the creek, which is narrower here but gurgling and lively, black and clear against the snow.

Then back into the hillside past the ancient burr oak, its lateral arms a reminder of the pre-settlement savanna when solitary oaks dotted the prairie. The old burr oaks spread their branches wide—no need to share the sun with a competing forest in those days. Today, the frost in the smallest branches is thick, the crystals sharp and pointed like needles.

In Wildcat Hollow we abandon the pre-set trail and stake out one of our own. It is tough going—more stepping than gliding with long skis—but it's an investment of sorts, a trust that other skiers will follow and pack down the trail.

Here, where the snow is fresh and untouched, I stab a ski pole as deeply as it will take, grind it about, and pull it back, the hole perfectly cylindrical and cavernous when I extract the pole. In this winter sunlight, the hole is glacier-blue, a hint of the depths where the mind can go in the deep, long sleep of winter.

The golf course behind my house provides a good, quick site for cross-country skiing. Other places offer more variety of trails leading in and out of woods, alongside creek beds, and across swinging bridges, but the golf course wins in proximity. I can carry my skis a block to get there; in a big snowstorm, I can put the skis on at my back door and glide down the side street and onto the course. I go in daylight or darkness, the moon my guide in the latter case.

But after a twelve-inch snowfall in February, the snow has become almost too deep to ski in, and I buy a pair of snowshoes to compensate. The snowshoes, I tell my wife, greatly increase the degree of miserable weather in which I can be outside. In late February, another nine inches fall, prefaced by a thick ice storm and followed by blizzard-like winds. It's time to test the theory.

It is 10 p.m. when I head out onto the course. I find, to my surprise, a single set of footprints, and follow them down into the valley. Curiously, they head directly to the first oak tree just beyond the fairway. Then shift north to the next oak, and west again to the next, always stopping at the base of the trunk.

I'm a little slow on the uptake until I realize that the only other creature that's been out here is a squirrel wandering from oak to oak. And I haven't even stashed any acorns.

There's always a payoff to a night like this, and tonight I find it in the stand of spruce on the hill to the south. Ice and heavy snow have weighted down the branches, and the gathering wind buffets them into slow, rhythmic bounces, like the bobbing manes of steeds pawing at a fence line. They are corals undulating in a deep, wet dark. I am the only one here. I am the only one seeing this.

Winter may be the deep sleep, but for me it is a sharpening of the senses. Hibernating creatures crawl deep into the den or cave and drift away: their heart rates drop to as low as four or five beats per minute, their body temperatures fall to 10 degrees above freezing. It's a low-energy existence, but they still draw down body fat gained through the summer and fall, or wake occasionally to a stash of nuts.

But my admiration lies with the creatures who tough it out: the deer who ambles through the woods, gnawing at twigs for the thin line of green beneath the woody bark (but stay out of my yard!); the squirrel who invents new ways to get at the bird feeder; the mouse who pokes through the snow to replenish his stash of seed; and the red-tailed hawk who spies him.

Every detail is precise and sharp on a sunny, bone-chilling morning following a snowfall. Gretel Ehrlich, in "The Smooth Skull of Winter," describes the sharpening effect of the quick cold on the mind:

> All winter we skate the small ponds—places that in summer are water holes for cattle and sheep—and here a reflection of mind appears, sharp, vigilant, precise. Thoughts, bright as frostfall, skate through our brains. In winter, consciousness looks like an etching.

The air is insubstantial (unlike summer, when the sky is a lake of humidity). What you see and what you hear is the thing itself: the snap of a branch in the woods; the towering column of rock un-cloaked by the death of the underbrush.

Is this bedrock stone-cold? Let it sleep.

"A day so cold it hurts to breathe; dry enough to freeze spit. . . . Spring seems far off, impossible, but it is coming. Already there is dusk instead of darkness at five in the afternoon; already hope is stirring at the edges of the day."

—Kathleen Norris, *Dakota*

A February hike with friends at White Pine Hollow, a 700-acre state forest in northeast Dubuque County. We climb a creek-side bank, six of us, to get to the largest stand of white pine in Iowa, some of them up to two-hundred-years-old. Descend past the tumbled car-sized boulders, cross Pine Creek, ascend again to find the rock tower, march past sinkholes, toss a stone into a vertical cave to hear it clatter, descend among the Castle Rocks where the snow has outlined the crevasses among the boulders.

We cross and re-cross Pine Creek half a dozen times, each time scouting for a sure foothold. I cross first to the sound of ice cracking beneath my boots, but I don't fall through. Good luck to the next attempt! The other hikers don't like the nature of my grin.

Downstream, the creek is open, and I try to find footholds among the stones, but come up short halfway across. "Here, try this!" my wife Dianne shouts, chuffing a big rock that lands within inches of where I stand and splashes me quite well. Payback.

I feel foolish later when we get stuck in the ice-coated parking lot. An hour and a farm tractor later we finally break free.

> Cold and chill, bless the Lord;
> Dew and rain, bless the Lord;
> Frost and cold, bless the Lord;
> Ice and snow, bless the Lord.
> —*Daniel* 3:67-70

A solitary early-March hike through the steep-bluffed woods of the Mines of Spain has become a tradition for me. I like hiking with friends and my wife, but sometimes I need a cobweb-clearing walk all alone.

The Mines of Spain is a fourteen-hundred-acre State Recreation Area just south of Dubuque, a designation that conjures up visions of speedboats and ATV trails but really means it is a wildlife refuge open for hunting in limited seasons. Named for the mining district that Julien Dubuque negotiated with both the Mesquakie and the Spanish Governor in 1797, the area later became a lead-mining free-for-all after the end of the Black Hawk War in 1832. After a few decades of mining, it slipped into a quieter existence: some farming on the ridge tops, a rock quarry near the Mississippi. The city took root just north of the Mines, which became state property in 1981.

With the help of the crampons on the bottoms of my snowshoes, I haul myself more or less straight up the steep-sloped 200-foot incline. Here on the ridge—just above where the soil balds away to bedrock— is a clearing in the woods that accentuates the ebbs and swells of the earth. Native American burial mounds dot these river hillsides unannounced, and I wonder if this is what I've found. Above the clearing, in the thick of the woods, lies a long and narrow rise in the snow—perhaps a linear burial mound or maybe just an abandoned pioneer fence line which has retained the soil that eroded from the fields on either side.

I'm not sure whether I am right about any of these speculations. I think about asking the DNR. But it really doesn't matter.

What matters most is the walk alone, through woods I haven't explored before, my thoughts at work and trying to read the story the land tells.

———————————————

Eventually—even for someone who celebrates winter—the cloudy skies feel like leaded weights. It is too much, too long. The color of winter is brown, white, and grey. In the woods, wet snow clings to the crotch of the oak, coats its branches like garland. Another grey day. I read once that the average color of the universe is beige. Pierced by the cardinal in the bush.

———————————————

Only a few days remain until the calendar says spring. That doesn't mean much around here, since we can get occasional snowfalls through April. March is traditionally our snowiest month, but I tell my wife, I wonder if that is based on the weather patterns of the past, as it doesn't seem to happen very often anymore. Still, late-season snowfalls are often quite heavy as cold Arctic air meets moisture-laden fronts crawling back up from the south.

As for today, it is 40 degrees outside, and the four-foot piles of snow along the driveway have been melting for days. Patches of brown earth are reappearing along the fence. We hear birds in the morning.

It may just be that winter is ending here.

Ice Age!

The last great continental glacier ground to its furthest reach twelve thousand years ago and retreated back to Greenland and northern Canada a mere ten thousand years ago, after having sculpted, bulldozed, and heaped rubble across much of North America, Europe, and northern Asia. The beast has been locked away ever since.

Ten thousand years. Ordinarily, geologists talk in terms of hundreds of millions of years ago, when limestone compacted under the weight of ancient seas or some vast comet pummeled the earth into mass extinctions. On the flip side, ten thousand years is just yesterday.

Try this. I am about fifty-years-old, and that has gone by in the blink of an eye. Count by fifty-year intervals, one per second, as your watch ticks away. Fifty-100-150-200, and so on. In one minute you will cover three thousand years. In three minutes and twenty seconds you will be at the glacier's retreating edge.

Chip off a block and put it in your drink.

Better yet, offer another chunk to the hunter eyeing you curiously from a safe distance. For humans have already arrived at the glacier's edge.

Then let the clock tick you quickly back to the present. We have business to attend to.

———————————

The final glaciers—dubbed the Wisconsinan—were just the latest in a string of twenty or so continental glaciers that crawled across much of the northern hemisphere in the past 2.5 million years.

All or most of the glaciers bypassed—slid west, east, and south of—my home in the Driftless Land, a twenty thousand square-mile swath along the Upper Mississippi Valley, leaving this land rugged and old.

I'd been spending my time recently learning about the Driftless Land. But to understand Driftless, I needed to know Drift.

I headed north in early April under a sunny sky, aiming to visit sites in northwest Wisconsin particularly rich in glacial features. There had been a hint of spring the day I left, winter having been stubborn and persistent until then. But as I neared northwest Wisconsin, the weather took a turn, first with drizzle, then flurries, and by the time I awoke the next morning in a hotel in the small town of Chetek, two inches of wet, sloppy snow had fallen, adding to the accumulation that still had not melted from the ditches and woods. Perhaps it was simply appropriate that my venture to see glacial deposits was accompanied by a spring snow squall.

I met Chippewa Moraine Ice Age Unit Naturalist Rod Gont the morning after the snowfall. The Visitors Center at Chippewa Moraine sits atop a small hill overlooking a prairie on one side and a deep woods behind. Gont's enthusiasm for explaining the ins and outs of glaciers was equaled only by my seemingly endless supply of questions. He immediately began turning my understanding of glaciers upside down.

Literally. For the hill we stood on, he pointed out, had been a low spot in the glacier—a glacial lake, to be precise. The surrounding lowlands had been high spots in the glacier. How did that work?

A low spot on the glacier accumulated debris—boulders, gravel, sand, and soil carried along in the ice—that had been thrust to the surface and then washed or settled into the low spots. Here at Chippewa Moraine, the depression had become an ice-walled lake, a lake situated within the now-melting glacier. The lake bottom accumulated sediment. Then, as the glacier melted down to the ground, the sediment that had been trapped in low spots and ice-walled lakes deposited out as hills (or hummocks) on the otherwise flattened landscape.

Everything within sight offered a glacial story, including the forested ridge just beyond the prairie. Chippewa Moraine marked the glacier's edge where the bottom ice was stagnant, as if glued to the ground beneath it. But even though the edge was no longer advancing, the center of the glacier kept pushing, thrusting new ice up over the old in piggy-back fashion, creating a jumbled surface. Boulders, rubble, and debris, picked up in the glacier's long scrape across Canada and Wisconsin, were thrust to the glacier's edge, and when the glacier melted, the debris deposited out and formed the moraine now visible as a line of forested hills.

The flatland plain I'd driven through when approaching Chippewa Moraine from the west was not glacial-sculpted as I'd first suspected, but rather outwash-sediments from the great melting.

And for my final upside-down experience, Gont led me down into the icy woods behind the Visitors Center. There in the bottomlands we found kettle lakes that had been high spots on the glacier. Of course.

Later, on my own, I found the hiking path that leads to and from Chippewa Moraine. The path is a segment of the still-in-development thousand-mile Ice Age Trail that will begin in northwest Wisconsin, strike eastward two-thirds of the way across the state, march south nearly to the Illinois border, and slip northeast again to Door County, following the furthermost edge of the Wisconsinan glacier. I hiked a half-mile or so through the mix of snow, ice, and standing meltwater, then decided to save the other 999 miles for later.

———————

The Wisconsinan period glaciers had merely been the latest. A period of glacial advances called the Illinoian ran from 130,000 to 300,000 BP ("before present"), outlining, as the name suggests, pretty much the present day shape of Illinois. It covered northern and eastern Wisconsin once again, but did not press into Iowa, except for a glancing blow to southeast Iowa along the Mississippi River.

Pre-Illinoian glaciers—sometimes divided into Nebraskan and Kansan—blanketed the northern states even earlier in periods from 500,000 to 2.5 million years BP. Some combination of these multiple glaciers covered most of Wisconsin, Minnesota, Iowa, and reached as far south as northern Missouri and Kansas. Whether northeast Iowa's thin crescent of the so-called Driftless Land (including my home in Dubuque) entirely escaped the more ancient glaciers seems doubtful according to recent studies, but I'll not lose sleep over it, as the landscape here mimics the rugged scenery of Wisconsin's and northwest Illinois' true driftless region.

What kept the glaciers away from the Driftless Land? Gont explains it in terms of the way that glaciers flow like liquid in slow motion. Much of northern Wisconsin is underlain by a hard igneous rock set down as lava when the Penokean Mountains rose above the ancient seas in northern Wisconsin 1.9 billion years ago. These ancient mountains wore down through erosion and perhaps early glaciation, but the hard, igneous bedrock remained in place. When the glacial ice scraped down from the north, it slid more easily into the lowlands to the east and west—now Lake Superior and Lake Michigan. The ice that did crawl across the hard igneous uplands lost momentum and stopped before reaching southwest Wisconsin.

Safe at a distance here in the Driftless Land, I like to imagine the glaciers in speeded-up motion. Can you feel the earth rumble as with a far-off train? Can you hear the snapping and crunching of ice in the distance? Has it finally crawled to a stop?

––––––––––

The imagination lets loose across the ice. Perhaps only metaphor captures the intensity of cold. Annie Dillard, in "An Expedition to the Pole," creates a nightmare of ice and emptiness, a migraine sharp as a pick-axe:

> My name is Silence. . . . My eyes are stones; a chip from the pack ice fills my mouth. My skull is a polar basin; my brain pan grows glaciers, and icebergs, and grease ice, and floes. The years are passing here.

For Gretel Ehrlich, in *The Future of Ice*, cold sharpens the mind and pulls us inward:

> The Japanese word *oku* means not only 'north' but also 'deep,' 'inner,' 'the heart of a mountain,' 'to penetrate to the depth of something or someone,' 'the bottom of one's heart,' and 'the end of one's mind.'

As for myself, I have wondered where the soul goes in a sterile, cold land. I have imagined, while driving across the flatlands, a mile of ice pressing down from above. I have wondered how slowly the seconds tick away across the ice.

What set off the great beasts from the north? While you can't trace the onset of the ice ages to some unfortunate alignment of the stars, the astronomical concept isn't totally off the mark. The earth's tilt cycles every 41,000 years between 22 to 25 degrees off vertical, and when the tilt is greatest, the north pole will be furthest away from the sun in winter. Winter deepens. In addition, the earth wobbles like a top through space, and every 22,000 years it completes a cycle, putting the north pole farther away from the sun. Winter deepens. Finally, the earth doesn't travel around the sun in a circle, but in an oval-shaped path, and when the hundred-thousand-year cycle takes the path farthest from the sun, winter deepens.

When all three cycles align and conspire, the great beast may awaken in the north.

Why not in the south? A perhaps not-so-obvious requirement for continental glaciers is the presence of continents. The southern hemisphere hasn't experienced widespread glaciers except, of course, for Antarctica, because there are few other large land masses close enough to the south pole for glaciers to crawl across.

Rod Gont knows a ton about glaciers, but he is not a showy man. When I cycled back at the end of our conversation to ask him if there was anything special he wanted to say about Chippewa Moraine where he works, he thought for a moment and said, no, except to add, "I like it here."

But as he tells you about glaciers, you can feel the cold (well, OK, we were deep in the wooded, snow-filled valley for a while, but that's not what I mean). You can feel the unfathomable pressure of the relentless ice.

The Wisconsinan glacier was 600 feet thick near its edge at the Chippewa Moraine, but farther back it was more than two miles deep over present-day Hudson Bay. It depressed the land surface at a ratio of one-third its thickness. The northern half of the continent has spent the past ten thousand years rebounding.

So much of the earth's water was tied up in the glaciers that sea levels fell 400 feet, opening up a land-path from Asia to Alaska (curiously un-glaciated) that humans followed in their incessant wanderlust. Many lingered at the glacier's edge, hunting mastodons and wooly mammoths until these mega fauna suffered perhaps the first human-induced extinctions. Other peoples dispersed through-out North and South America, the ancestors of Native Americans, the first immigrants to the New World.

———————

The ice in my driveway this winter seemed solid as a stone at the curb where I'd given up trying to melt and chop it down to the concrete. The ice on my roof seemed immobile, until during a slight thaw it let loose and pulled the gutter down with it.

How then, on a flat plain, does ice begin to crawl?

When snow survives the summer melt, as it did when the world grew colder, it compacts into ice and receives the next year's snow, which in turn compacts during the following summer's partial melt. At a hundred-foot depth, after centuries of accumulation, the ice begins to flow like heated plastic, at first perhaps molding itself to the contours of the land, but then—as it gains weight, depth, and force—gouging, scraping, shoveling the land before it. In one place, it might crawl along at a few meters per year. Somewhere else the ice might advance one or two kilometers per year. At its final reach, where summer melt offsets the push of new ice, the glacier's edge doesn't move at all, but the ice behind still presses forth. Stalemate.

Ninety thousand years ago, the Wisconsinan glacial period began, with numerous retreats and advances along the way. Twenty thousand years ago, it began its final assault. The earth's annual average temperature dropped by six degrees. Back in the center of the glacier, the average temperatures plunged by twenty.

The ice pressed southward in competing lobes like rivulets extending from a spill.

Among them, the Lake Michigan lobe and the Green Bay lobe competed for eastern Wisconsin, piling a line of hilly moraines between them from Door County nearly to the Illinois border. The Chippewa lobe ended at the forested ridge Rod Gont pointed to from the Visitors Center at Chippewa Moraine. The Superior lobe pressed into northwest Wisconsin. The Des Moines lobe pushed through Minnesota and took a bite out of north and central Iowa.

———————

Can you calculate a tipping point? With enough data, a physicist will know when the books I've stacked on my desk will topple. With less accuracy, and perhaps only with hindsight, the psychologist may know when the young man went bad. When did the summer grow warm enough and the winter less intense so that the ice groaned to a halt and then began its slow retreat? About twelve thousand years ago the glacier began receding.

But was it on a Tuesday in April?

———————

It was warming slightly when I left Chippewa Moraine, passed through the plains of the glacial outwash, crossed briefly through the hilly northwest corner of the Driftless Land, and then entered again into another flatlands glaciated by the Superior lobe, en route to Interstate Park at St. Croix Falls along the Wisconsin-Minnesota border, where I intended to view effects of the great glacial melt. I read the landscape as I drove.

Landscape always tells a story. At Interstate Park the story is about potholes. Not potholes like the ones in Dubuque streets that wreaked havoc on car alignments this winter. But curious rounded holes in the thick basalt carved by swishing boulders during the meltdown.

Backing up way more than three minutes on the ticking clock, lava erupted in Interstate Park 1,100 million years BP through cracks in the earth's surface. The cracks followed a fault line from Lake Superior to Iowa as the North American continent briefly considered splitting apart. The erupting lava formed the hard, dark-grey basalt bedrock of today's park.

High up in the basalt bluffs—up to 100 feet above the St. Croix River—you will find the kettle-shaped potholes. They may be as small as a foot across and deep, or as large as fifteen by sixty. The potholes formed when Glacial Lake Duluth—predecessor to Lake Superior— burst as the glaciers were melting. The meltwater rushed down the St. Croix River, gouged out Taylor Falls, and swirled boulders of many sizes in monstrous eddies. These swirling boulders bore into the hard basalt bedrock like drill bits, forming potholes that became part of the bluff when the glacial melt dissipated and the St. Croix became a small, albeit impressive, river once again in the downcut valley. Some of the culprit boulders have even been found at the bottom of the potholes, like ancient bowling balls.

———————————

Maybe the ticking intensifies. There is something in the air as meltwater drips from the glacier's edge. Does it seem warmer to you this summer?

———————————

It isn't everlasting winter on the glacier, nor is it blindingly white. Boulders, rubble, and wind-blown loess lie thick in patches. Some-times the loess is deep enough to grow a tundra grass on top of the ice. The sun warms in the summer, and ice melts. Meltwater carves holes in the ice and plunges within, forming winding passageways deep inside or at its base. When the runoff slows—at winter's return or the demise of the glacier—sediment drops to the earthen floor, forming little winding hills like s-curves, called eskers.

Sometimes the glacier acts as a dam against rivers flowing toward it. The Wisconsin River meanders in a southerly flow before turning southwest on its way to the Mississippi. The Green Bay lobe creeps in and blocks its southerly flow. They wrestle for a while, before the blocked river backs up and forms Glacial Lake Wisconsin, stretching seventy miles north to south from Wisconsin Rapids to Wisconsin Dells and thirty miles east to west from the Dells to Camp Douglas, where the Mill Bluff rock towers are islands near the lake shore.

Eventually the ice dam breaks as the climate warms, sending the Wisconsin River surging on its path, accompanied by a hellish spring flood as Glacial Lake Wisconsin drains in a matter of weeks.

In south-central Wisconsin, competing glacial lobes block off a deep, ancient gorge at two ends with moraines, and the melting ice leaves behind Devil's Lake with 500-foot outcroppings above the lake. Another glacial lake in northeast Wisconsin drains quickly as the ice recedes, leaving behind Horicon Marsh, today a 32,000 acre wildlife refuge of particular value to migratory waterfowl.

After the swelling rivers carry silt and sand outwash away from the glaciers and deposit it on their floodplains, the winds take over and disperse the fine loess dust throughout the Midwest, providing the basis for fertile farm soils. In western Iowa, the winds sweep the floodplain silt into dune-like swells called the Loess Hills in a narrow band stretching two hundred miles north to south along the Missouri River. The deposits range from 60 to 200 feet deep.

While the seconds tick away, North America is remade.

On the drive back from northwest Wisconsin, I feel at home when the sharp bluffs and valleys of the Driftless present themselves again. The spring snow squall has intensified, and the limestone outcroppings in the woods bare themselves against the bleak backdrop of brown and white.

Ten thousand years ago I live among the hills on the Mississippi, where Dubuque now stands. The winters have been mind-numbingly cold, but there is no glacier here. Maybe I am the tribal storyteller. Maybe I weave an ancient story about lands not far to the north with ice so thick the ground is never seen. Maybe someone in the tribe doesn't believe it.

The summers grow warmer, the winters less intense.

The glacier to the north is melting! Runoff pours into the river directly from Minnesota, sweeps down the Wisconsin River, gorges the Yellow River and other tributaries, all joining the Mississippi, which grows wilder by the day, churning, running brim to brim from bluff to bluff, every summer for hundreds of years.

The storming Mississippi cuts even deeper, as its sides are hemmed in by bluffs in the Driftless Land. When the meltwaters are finished, there will be 250 feet of glacial till at the river bottom, testimony to how deep the Mississippi once flowed.

But that still lies in the future. For now, the storyteller convinces the doubtful: "The ice is melting. See how the river rages?"

It is perhaps inevitable that all this talk of ice ages leads us back to the present. Your three minutes and twenty seconds are up.

We are, in the technical sense, still within the boundaries of the ice age, as continental glaciers still blanket Greenland and other high latitudes, and perch on the slopes of high-altitude mountains. But they are quickly receding. Greenland is calving ice into the Atlantic at double its former rate and has been losing thirty-six cubic miles of ice per year since the turn of the century. In March of 2008, the twenty-six-square-miles Wilkins Ice Shelf in Antarctica collapsed into the ocean in a region where average annual temperatures have increased almost a degree per decade for the past fifty years. Photographs of mountain glaciers across the world show a nearly steady retreat throughout the past century, and Glacier National Park may soon be without any. Twenty of the twenty-one hottest years in global temperature since the Civil War have occurred since 1980.

This time the beast might not be the ice, but the meltwater. If half of the Greenland and Antarctica glaciers melt, sea levels could rise almost twenty feet, wiping out low-lying coastal cities and sending their populations packing across the world.

The doubtful ones in the tribe question whether global warming actually exists, or whether it is a natural occurrence, or whether its impact will be as bad as predicted, or whether there is anything we can do about it even if it is underway.

True, the world may toggle over into a slow decrease or slow increase in temperature on its own, thank you, which, given time, unleashes the great beasts of ice or meltwater. But the current speed of climate change is too pronounced for that. The culprit this time is carbon dioxide in the atmosphere, not the rare meshing of the earth's rotational cycles.

The skeptics in the tribe scratch their heads and calculate the economic costs of reducing the carbon footprint.

Meanwhile, the clock is ticking.

Sacred Place:
The Landscape of Memory

*Brother wind and sister water, mother
earth and father sky, Sacred plants and
sacred creatures, sacred people of the land.*
—Marty Haugen, "Song At the Center"

I remember it years later, plain as day, although it was, in fact, night. We were returning to our vacation campsite in the South Dakota Black Hills about two hours past sunset, our children then ages seventeen, fourteen, and eleven. We still had half an hour to drive on the wildlife road that winds through Custer State Park. In the distance I could make out the taillights of a minivan stopped on the road. We quickly learned why.

Hundreds of buffalo were crossing the road from the right. They were deep, black shadows darker than the night, and then one by one they passed into the headlights of the van in front of us. For the few moments it took them to trot across the road, they were illuminated—big snorting bulls, powerful cows, and a smattering of skittering calves. And then they'd pass out of the headlights and back into the night shadow, until the last bull brought up the rear and disappeared with the herd up onto a hill at the left.

Then the show was apparently over. The van in front of us moved on and so did we. But fifty yards later, the van slowed again, and the show resumed with the herd lunging down off the hill to the left, passing through the headlights a second time and into the shadows at the right. But this time, while the main pack was still passing before us, the front of the herd began swooping up behind. Buffalo to the front, buffalo to the rear—we were encircled by buffalo!

The second act ended quickly, too. The herd tired of the game, satisfied their curiosity, or finally decided where they wanted to bed down for the night. And we headed back to the campsite to bed down as well.

Nothing spectacular had happened, nothing horrific. And I have never forgotten a single detail.

———————————

I carry in my mind an even older photograph, more than twenty years old, of a clear November sky. My wife and I had been hiking in the bluffs along the Mississippi River with our first child, Paul—still a baby—perched in a carrier on my back. We'd started on the valley floor at Catfish Creek in the Mines of Spain State Recreation Area near our home in Dubuque, Iowa, followed a trail up into the woods past remnants of century-old lead-mine pits, through thickets of overgrown forest, into a cedar grove, and then turned a corner—a glorious turn—to find bare white branches from a stand of birch etching themselves sharply against a brilliant blue sky. It was the kind of pale blue that whispers to your bones that it's the last warm day of autumn, not the deeper shade of blue that drips with sweat in summer. It was a blue so thin that it couldn't hold up a cloud.

We'd left the camera home, so I told myself that memory would have to suffice. I haven't forgotten the image.

———————————

I was thinking the other day about the memories we carry, the kind that don't require a camera but burn themselves into our souls. The big events are easy, perhaps even trivial in the scheme of things: graduations, weddings, births of children. To the contrary, the plainer moments form the landscape of memory. The family all-night card party in my parents' kitchen when, at dawn, Uncle Norb proclaimed with startling clarity that the coffee we'd been drinking for hours tasted "like shit" and set us doubling over with laughter. The scout camping trip with the boys in November when I forsook the tent and climbed inside the pickup's covered topper and listened to muffled soft clumps of wet first-snow descending for hours through the night.

The landscape of memory gives birth to the sense of "place." My family kitchen, the city I live in, the river bluffs along the Upper Mississippi in the Driftless Land, even the places I've visited only briefly, all take form from layers of memory. Mine, yours, and the dead and gone. The deeper the layering, the richer the place. Walter Brueggemann, in *The Land*, writes:

> Place is space which has historical meanings, where some things have happened which are now remembered and which provide continuity and identity across generations. Place is space in which important words have been spoken which have established identity.

Or, as Philip Sheldrake puts it, in *Spaces for the Sacred*: "Place depends on relationships and memories as much as on physical features." The blufftops along the river where I frequently hike are awash in old, spent conversations, not to mention the rusting barbed-wire fences of past farmsteads and the silent, hidden presence of Native American burial mounds. The bird dusting snow off the feeder in the yard next door takes my thoughts immediately to my neighbors, Mark and Ginger, and the conversations we've had over the fence, and how they've watched our children grow. Space becomes "place" when bestowed with meaning.

Alternatively, I can speed down an interstate—as I have—taking no notice of the land and not even reading the names of the towns bypassed, and imbue no sense of place at all on where I've been. I can spend all day in virtual space and never make physical contact, forfeiting again the chance to connect to place.

Place is space that has been contemplated.

But we spend much of our lives as if enveloped in cotton, with the world distant, muffled, and blurred. As the saying goes—and it is true—I may remember the buffalo and the birches from years ago, but I can't remember what I had for lunch yesterday. Life gets busy, responsibilities pile up, and our cultural tendency toward excess crowds out awareness of the world. Still, the nineteenth-century American transcendentalist Ralph Waldo Emerson told us to be a "transparent eye," taking in all things. Contemporary author Annie Dillard implores us to empty the mind, to quell the ongoing chatter between the ears, to be fully aware in the present moment.

———————————

I once spent twenty-four hours visiting New Melleray Abbey, near Dubuque. I was preparing to teach a new course, called Monastery Voices, and I thought a twenty-four-hour stint with the Trappists would lend validity and authenticity. Such as it were. I would be alone with my thoughts in the Guesthouse. I would go to the chapel seven times to watch the monks file in—grey and bent with age, most of them. I would read. I would write.

I remember this: I took a walk in the single-digit chill of a January afternoon. Across the road lay a country Catholic church where my aunt and uncle were parishioners and where they'd hosted some lazy summer family reunions. Now under the chill of winter, I wandered through the cemetery, pondering the Irish immigrant pioneers who'd thrown in their lot next door to the Irish monks and who'd already racked up a century of sleep in their smallish plot of prairie real estate.

And I remember this: At 3:30 a.m. I joined the monks for Vigils, the first gathering of the day. The empty chapel was dark, save for a single orange-colored light suspended above the altar. The light shone as the monks shuffled in one by one, shone above their chanting voices, shining forever, as it were, a rising and setting sun shining forever and ever, amen. I remember that.

Trappists, or Cistercians, are an offshoot of the Benedictines and follow the Rule of Saint Benedict. The Rule requires that, among other things, "They will regard all utensils and goods of the monastery as sacred vessels of the altar, aware that nothing is to be neglected" (RB 31:10-12). What I love about the Benedictines is their sense of metaphor trumping literalism. It's not just the monastery tools and goods that are sacred here. Joan Chittister, OSB, takes the

Rule out of the monastery and interprets it for the broader world, imploring us, in a word, to "awareness":

> In Benedictine Spirituality, everything is sacred and every-thing is one. . . . Awareness of the sacred in life is what holds our world together and the lack of awareness and sacred care is what is tearing it apart. We have covered the earth with con-crete and wonder why children have little respect for the land.

Sacred land. The word "sacred" conjures up cathedrals, mosques, temples, cemeteries, burial mounds, and Holy Lands walked upon by Jesus, Mohammed, and Buddha. The word will empower some people and chase others away. But consider the roots of the word "sacred." Its long etymological history says the sacred is that which protects us and binds us—to each other and to the land. Moreover, the story of "sacred" includes the story of "sacrum," a bone at the bot-tom of the spine, an earthy, profane term if ever there were one.

Sacred is within our bones, it is our holy bones, it is the rock and bone of the physicality of earth made holy. Turn it into Christianity or Druidism or Islam if you will, but at base it is the sense that there is more to this place than physicality. A layering of memory and meaning swirls about a place like a fine mist, if you move slowly enough through it to be aware. That is sacred place.

In *Landscapes of the Sacred*, Belden C. Lane explains that sacred ground is more often located in the ordinary than in the extreme. The sacred mountain of the Himalayas, he points out, is Mount Kailas, not Mount Everest. Jerusalem is not the grandest, tallest mound of Palestine. Henry David Thoreau found intimations of God in the relatively humble surroundings of Walden Pond and its surrounding woods. Kathleen Norris finds her "monastery" in the plains of the Dakotas, where God can be seen in the details of grasshopper and long-stem prairie, and the eye is not distracted by grandeur. The sacred is diffused throughout nature, yet paradoxically it tends to gather in select places, almost as if drawn by gravity. "The heritage of Romanticism," says Lane, "has conditioned us to expect the holy place to be marked by excessive beauty and grandeur," but the sacred does the choosing, not us, and by masking itself in the ordinary, it forces us to look closely at our world, to see it for more than it appears, to realize that the sacred is not apart from the profane.

Even so, I chafe at the implication that one plot is sacred and another not. Perhaps, like mist, the sacred shifts and roils, flows into the valley and lifts again, visits here, then there, and returns again throughout the landscape of memory.

———————————————

There is still one more story imprinted on my memory from that Black Hills family vacation. We went off the beaten path at least once, on a four-hour round-trip hike up to and down from Mount Harney, the highest point east of the Rocky Mountains. Our young daughter Angie complained about the long hike, but she trekked it just like the rest of us. When we arrived at the summit, our son Brian climbed atop the domed rock at the very top, just beyond my sight (I being too chicken to follow him). The wind at that height howled so loudly that he couldn't hear me when I called to him to come back after several minutes, and I, having lost sight of him, began to worry that he had fallen.

Later I learned that Black Elk had had his famous shamanistic visions on that very ground, at what he called the center of the world. It too is sacred place.

But near the domed summit of Mount Harney is another vantage point, an old abandoned fire tower that I could climb. From here I could see what Brian had seen from the dome. From the fire tower I could see that this sacred place is connected inch by inch and mile by mile, summit by summit and valley by valley, connected across the plains and the rivers and the cities, back to the Driftless Land where I live and to every other square inch of earth, and it is all sacred land.

Such is the landscape of memory.

Chasing Black Hawk

*Rock River was a beautiful country; I
loved my towns, my cornfields, and the
home of my people. I fought for it.*
—Black Hawk, 1832

We were digging out from yet another winter storm in a season
inching toward a record snowfall. This had been perhaps the season's
worst dump, not in inches, but in the tenacity of the freezing rain that
coated the streets and highways before the snow began falling. Making matters worse, communities were running low on road salt. It
was—even to this lover of winter—a mess.

Thus I began my three-day chase of Black Hawk, a trek I'd been
planning for some time ever since the ninetheenth-century Sauk and
his cause had captured my fancy.

You can't live in the middle of the Midwest—Iowa, Illinois,
Wisconsin—without hearing the name Black Hawk. You'll find
Black Hawk County in East-Central Iowa, Black Hawk Community
College in Moline, Illinois, Black Hawk High School in South Wayne,
Wisconsin, innumerable Black Hawk parks and recreation areas and
businesses, and, of course, the Chicago Blackhawks hockey team, just
to name a few. But for the most part, it is just another name, devoid
of a particular context.

In a sense, it is an old, oft-repeated story. The nineteenth-century
Native American tribe is driven from its homeland by the American
government, a renegade band tries to reclaim the homeland, led by

a fierce and charismatic warrior, and the whole bloody scene ends in massacre and further removal to even more remote lands. It's just that this particular rendition took place in my own backyard, and my own roots wouldn't be complete if I didn't know the story deeply enough.

I'd known bits and pieces about the Black Hawk War for a long, long time, but it didn't hit home until a few years ago when I happened upon a historical marker on State Highway 35 along the Mississippi River in southwest Wisconsin. I'd been admiring the 400-foot river bluffs and steeply carved, bisecting valleys, pulling over to the roadside for frequent photos, when suddenly I came face-to- face with the past in the form of a monument announcing the place of massacre where the Bad Axe River enters the Mississippi. So here is where it ended, I thought, some 200 miles upriver from Black Hawk's home, some 550 miles after the trek began.

Why so much blood amid this beauty?

To tell it briefly: In 1829, the United States Government forced all Sauk and Mesquakie living in northwestern Illinois and southwestern Wisconsin to move west of the Mississippi, where they had already established some villages and where they frequently spent their winter hunt. Of particular loss was the village of Saukenuk, at the current location of Rock Island, Illinois, at the mouth of the Rock River along the Mississippi. The Sauk warrior Black Hawk rejected the counsel of acquiescing chiefs and garnered a renegade band of between 1,000 to 1,500 warriors, women, children, and elderly, who re-crossed the river in attempt to resettle their former lands. The warriors among them engaged in a handful of battles and skirmishes with U.S. forces, but soon even the women, children, and elderly found themselves scrambling up the Rock River and then—in final desperation—back toward the Mississippi in a 550-mile trek, pursued by the U.S. Army and the Illinois Volunteer Militia. The government troops, ever a day late and miles behind, eventually knew they were honing in on the Sauk when they found signs of starvation along the trail. At first it was the stripped tree bark and the uprooted, vile tubers, but eventually it was the weak and the lame they overtook and—not knowing what to do with them—killed.

At the Mississippi it turned out badly, just south of the ominously named Bad Axe River.

———————————————————

I'd often wondered about the whole ill-fated affair. I'd often wondered about the curious juxtaposition of the beautiful lands that Black Hawk and his people had lived in and passed through, and how that beauty must have mixed with blood and fear during the summer of 1832. I'd often thought about following the path myself.

Setting out to trace the Black Hawk trail by car was cheesy, but I live in a world of work, family, and modern comfort where hoofing it on foot for four months was simply not an option.

Setting out in the aftermath of the winter's worst storm was an accident of the calendar. I'm not a foolish man, nor a risk-taker. This was simply when I had blocked out some time to travel. Two days after the storm had passed, I thought the roads would be cleared and safe. But for the first twenty-five miles heading south out of my home in Dubuque, Iowa, I gripped the steering wheel tightly, turned off the CD player, sat at the edge of my seat, and plodded down the frozen highway at thirty miles an hour, gaping at the dozens of abandoned cars and semis still in the median and ditches—one flipped on its roof—and calculated the safest place to turn around and try again another day.

Finally I decided on the town of Maquoketa—thirty miles south—as the next place with an interchange where I might more safely turn around. But as I neared the town, the highway cleared to the south, and in the end it struck me that by now it was safer to just keep going than to drive back through the mess from which I'd just emerged. That held true . . . for a while.

Still, it occurred to me after the fact that this deep winter excursion in below-zero wind chills and icy roads was in some small way an act of solidarity with Black Hawk and his band, if only in the sense of sharing a bit of discomfort. We don't, in the modern world, handle

inconvenience and discomfort well, unless you disregard the incap-
acitated swimming pool at my first hotel. But I'm getting ahead of
myself.

———————————

The Sauk and Mesquakie[1]—considered "cousin" tribes—were
relatively recent newcomers to the lands on either shore of the upper
Mississippi and Wisconsin Rivers. The seventeenth century had seen
them driven out by the French and Indian Wars from their wooded
homeland along the St. Lawrence River near present-day Montreal
into Ontario, and then chased by the Iroquois south along Wisconsin's Fox River and eventually to the upper Mississippi, where they
arrived in the mid-1700s. The Mesquakie settled in several villages,
including one near the present location of Dubuque on the Mississippi. The more numerous Sauk settled in three villages just slightly
south along the river.

Saukenuk, the largest of the three villages and located on the
eastern shore along the Rock River (or Sinissippi), would have been
impressive by historical terms. Home to 4,800 Sauk by 1826, the village boasted numerous fifty-foot dwelling lodges, a public square,
and a council house. Beyond the settlement lay eight hundred acres
of cultivated farmland, tallgrass prairie for horses, and gardens of
berries, apples, and plums.

The village was, you might say, a three-seasons home to the Sauk.
In spring they planted their gardens; in summer the young men went
off for the bison hunt and the women and older men caught and
dried fish; and in fall came the harvest and celebratory games. Along
the way they held various feasts, such as the Crane Dance Festival
in which villagers put on their finest clothes, and young men and
women were paired up for marriage. Occasional battles broke out
with the nearby Sioux and Ioway.

Late September saw an exodus by small bands into the surrounding plains for winter hunting and trapping. But even though the
harvests were impressive with corn and pumpkins and squash, the

———————————

1. The Sauk and Mesquakie were often known, in earlier times, as the Sac and
Fox Indians.

Saukenuk villagers were not entirely self-sufficient. Before the Winter Hunt, European-American traders would ply them with goods on credit—guns, metal tools, traps, cooking pots, and the like. The traders followed them out into the winter prairie and set up shop at a convenient remove, collecting skins and dried meats as they accumulated. When April arrived, the clans returned to Saukenuk for a final settling up with the traders. As game became more scarce on the plains, the Sauk fell deeper into debt.

Into this setting was born Ma-katai-me-she-kia-kiak, or Black Sparrow Hawk, around 1767. A warrior who travelled and battled extensively, he loved his home village. In his autobiography he wrote: "We always had plenty—our children never cried with hunger, nor our people were never in want. Here our village had stood for more than a hundred years, during all which time we were the undisputed possessors of the valley of the Mississippi, from the Ouisconsin [Wisconsin River] to the Portage des Sioux, near the mouth of the Missouri, being about seven hundred miles in length."

I had actually begun my own chase of Black Hawk the previous October when I drove to Rock Island, Illinois, to view the Black Hawk State Historical Site on the hills overlooking the valley where Saukenuk had been situated, eighty miles south of my home. A small patch of tallgrass prairie reminded visitors what the rolling lands beyond the river valley looked like in the early 1800s before succumbing to the plow. In contrast, the bluffs along the Mississippi were heavily wooded with oaks and maples. The two-hundred-acre Black Hawk Forest Nature Preserve, one of the "least-disturbed forests in Illinois," was leaf-strewn at this mid-autumn phase.

Like many Midwestern woods, this forest had now grown crowded with scrub trees in the intervening years since prairie fires would have blown through and exacted a thorough cleansing, but here and there were remnants of the ages. Here an eighty-foot oak with a five-foot circumference might have seen the days of Saukenuk; there an ancient fallen oak—eight feet of its stump still intact and notched by woodpeckers—might have known Black Hawk himself. A few purple wildflowers still managed to poke through the crowded forest floor in October.

In the bluffs above the river there once lay two-thousand-year-old burial mounds of Hopewellian peoples who long predated the Sauk. The mounds are no longer intact.

Below the historical site, in the flatlands near the river—the actual location of Saukenuk—lay an aging commercial and residential district of the city of Rock Island. There is not much there to remind you of the former time. Here is the Rock River. And there—lest you miss it—is the Blackhawk TV store and the Blackhawk Apartments.

It was here that I was born—and here lie the bones of many friends and relations. For this spot I felt a sacred reverence, and never could consent to leave it, without being forced therefrom.
—Black Hawk, *An Autobiography*

European-Americans, too, had been impressed with the Sauk village and its surroundings. In 1829, U.S. Indian Commissioner Caleb Atwater described the lands around the mouth of the Rock River: "At every turn of the river . . . bursts of wonder and admiration were poured out by the passengers. [The woods were] thick, lofty, green and delightful." The prairie left him "in breathless silence several minutes, looking on this diluvial plain, absorbed in deep contemplation."

Saukenuk had quickly come under the watchful eye of the young American government. The Sauk had favored the British during the American War of Independence, and as a result, American troops burned the village in 1780 in the westernmost campaign of the war, but the Sauk returned and rebuilt. General Zebulon Pike visited the Sauk village in 1805 as he worked his way north[2] taking notes on the river and the Native American settlements. While at Saukenuk, he

------

2. Pike's next stop would be at Julien Dubuque's Mines of Spain, at Dubuque. There he unsuccessfully peppered the French-Canadian Dubuque with questions about his mining operation (never tell too much to the tax man). Before his departure, Sauk canoeists arrived from downriver with two of Pike's explorers he'd managed to leave behind.

offered an American flag to replace the British Union Jack, but the Sauk demurred and merely flew it alongside. When the Sauk again sided with the British in the War of 1812, the U.S. government soon thereafter built Fort Armstrong on an island in the Mississippi, just five miles above Saukenuk, to keep an eye on things.

Already by Rock Island the tall bluffs that line the Mississippi further north have begun to tame themselves. They are smaller, more rounded here, a bit muted compared to my home in Dubuque. Still, the bluffs provide breathtaking views of the wide expanse of river. But just beyond the bluffs, the flatlands of western Illinois begin. These are the lands laid level by the multiple Illinoian-period glaciers of 130,000 to 300,000 years ago, glaciers that helped shape the state's boundaries by setting the paths of the Mississippi and Ohio Rivers near the glaciers' edge.

Glaciers are slow-moving behemoths, but perhaps the stones could hear them coming, coming.

The historical events that led to the Black Hawk War were fraught with advances and retreats. Already by 1804 a contingent of Sauk— unauthorized travelers acting on their own accord—had signed the Treaty of St. Louis ceding Sauk and Mesquakie lands east of the Mississippi in exchange for cash and supplies. But the Sauk signers later swore they believed the treaty had not included lands above the Rock River, thus sparing their beloved Saukenuk. And since the treaty did not require the Sauk to leave their lands until they were sold to settlers, the Sauk lived on at their village well into the 1820s, reinforcing their belief that Saukenuk would remain their home.

By 1828, however, the pressure of westward-moving traders, farmers, miners, and merchants was growing intense, and U.S. Agents warned the Sauk that they would have just one year until they must move west across the Mississippi. When Black Hawk returned to Saukenuk early from the winter hunt in Iowa in 1829, he found white settlers illegally occupying parts of the village, fencing off fields for their own spring planting. Black Hawk appealed unsuccessfully to the Indian agent at Fort Armstrong to have the squatters removed. Meanwhile, another Sauk warrior, Keokuk, convinced a majority of the Sauk of the wisdom of doing as the White Man required, i.e., of remaining on the west bank of the river.

Again in 1830, Black Hawk and his followers—dubbed by Americans as "the British band"—attempted to return to Saukenuk and plant corn, but found the village almost completely occupied by whites, still illegally, as most of the land had not actually been sold. Crops that the returning Sauk women planted nearby were later ploughed under by the whites, leading to a dire winter.

In spring of 1831, Black Hawk and his band returned one more time, but as June rolled around, the Illinois Militia was summoned to remove them. First, however, the Army's Major Edmund P. Gaines rode ahead of the Militia and tried one last time at Fort Armstrong to convince the Sauk to abandon the village. For the moment, Black Hawk capitulated, reluctantly signing an agreement to never return to the east side of the Mississippi.

But such was not in Black Hawk's heart: "My reason teaches me that *land cannot be sold*. The Great Spirit gave it to his children to live upon, and cultivate, as far as is necessary for their subsistence; and so long as they occupy and cultivate it, they have the right to the soil—but if they voluntarily leave it, then any other people have a right to settle upon it."

When the Militia arrived at Saukenuk, they found the village deserted, and burned it.

You can feel the tension in the cabin as Major Gaines upbraids the warrior who is not even a chief, yet has led his band of Sauk across the Mississippi in defiance of the orders to evacuate Saukenuk. "Who is *Black Hawk*? Who is *Black Hawk*?"

"I am a Sac! my forefather was a Sac! and all the nations call me a Sac!"

Gaines cuts to the quick: "I came here, neither to *beg* nor *hire* you to leave your village. My business is to remove you, peaceably if I can, but *forcibly* if I must!"[3]

How smooth must be the language of the whites, when they can make right look like wrong, and wrong like right
—Black Hawk, *An Autobiography*

In the fall of 1831, Black Hawk's chief advisor, Neapope, returns from consultations and reports from conversations with a nearby Winnebago chief known as The Prophet[4] that neighboring tribes— the Potawatomi, Ojibwe, Ottawa, and Winnebago[5]—and even the British up in Canada!—will support the Sauk if they return to live peacefully along the Rock River.

With these assurances, Black Hawk convinces over a thousand Sauk—warriors, women, children, and elderly—to cross the river once again, on April 5, 1832, to resettle their village along the Rock River or to resettle further upstream. The rest of the tribe remains with Keokuk. The band sets out from Keokuk's village about a hundred miles south of Saukenuk on the Mississippi at the mouth of the Des Moines River.

Very soon the mission begins to go bad. Hearing that U.S. Army reinforcements have arrived and an Illinois Militia has been formed to force them back across the river, Black Hawk and his band bypass Saukenuk and head forty miles northeast up the Rock River to the Prophet's Village, to await reinforcements, which, for the most part, fail to materialize.

Meanwhile, the U.S. Army, led by General Henry Atkinson, follows in slow pursuit. Thus far, Atkinson reasons, Black Hawk has committed no violence, and the possibility still exists to end the matter peacefully.

---

3. From *Black Hawk: An Autobiography*, pp. 111-112.
4. Wabokieshiek.
5. Now conventionally known as the Ho-Chunk

Black Hawk, dispirited by the lack of support at the Prophet's Village and knowing of the Army's pursuit, reluctantly decides it is not possible to fight for his lands. But knowing that he is being pursued, he pushes onward up the Rock River in order to avoid a conflict.

General Atkinson's army has 340 regulars. But the Governor of Illinois has raised a Militia of 1,700 Volunteers under the charge of General Samuel Whiteside to aid in the army's quest. Atkinson holds back, waiting for supplies, but allows Whiteside's militia to push on ahead, with orders to "move upon him, and either make him surrender at discretion or coerce him into submission."

But first the Indian Agent Henry Gratiot rushes to the Prophet's Village to try to reason with Black Hawk on April 24. Tension is thick as the Sauk lower Gratiot's white flag and raise the British flag in its place. Black Hawk tells Gratiot that Sauk and Fox "hearts are bad" and will fight if Atkinson pursues. Gratiot is taken hostage, but the Prophet intervenes, giving Gratiot enough time to flee in a canoe.

The Sauk pick up camp and move again further northeast along the Rock River. The Prophet and his small band of Winnebago go with him.

On May 10, Whiteside's militia enters the abandoned Prophet's Village and burns it.

The wind whips across open frozen fields as I cross into Illinois en route to Prophetstown, but the roads are clear. The brunt of the storm had passed in an arc to the north, although the flatland fields are coated in a hard-scrabble ice.

The town of 2,100 was founded in 1834, just two years after the Black Hawk War.

I pull into town on State Highway 78, looking for some sign of the Prophet. To the left is Prophet-Gear; down the road a retirement village, Prophet Manor. I drop in at the Prophetstown Echo newspaper office and inquire about historical information, hoping for a brochure or a booklet. "It's easier to get from the internet," the receptionist suggests. At the local gas station I ask whether there is a historical marker in town. "You might try down at the Veterans Park," the cashier suggests.

The marker is at the city park instead, its base encased in the overwhelming ice. I repeatedly blow warm breath on my pen's tip to unfreeze it in the 15-below-zero wind chills in order to record the signboard's message: "Prophetstown occupies the site of the village of the Winnebago Prophet, which the Illinois Volunteers destroyed on May 10, 1832, in the first act of hostility in the Black Hawk War.

Or maybe not the first. On Friday, May 9, Sauk warriors burn the trading post of Stephen Mack, Jr. Local Winnebagoes step in to spare Mack's life.

Militia are popping up with the greening grasses. General Atkinson commissions Henry Dodge to gather a force of Volunteers from today's Iowa County in southwest Wisconsin of the Michigan Territory to be ready if Black Hawk continues north. The Illinois Governor commissions Isaiah Stillman to gather another force of Volunteers, who maneuver to within eight miles of Black Hawk's camp. More than two thousand government forces are now on the plains.

On May 14, Black Hawk sends three Sauk with a white flag toward Stillman's camp, but shrewdly sends another five observers to linger behind and watch what transpires. Stillman's scouts sight the truce flags, but then spot the observers and believe it is ambush. They shoot and kill one of the flag bearers and pursue the observers, who escape to warn Black Hawk, who in turn responds with a forty-warrior charge near nightfall that sends Stillman's men fleeing in panic, racing to Dixon's Ferry to regroup. The event will be known ignobly as Stillman's Run.

"I had resolved upon giving up the war—and sent a *flag of peace*, said Black Hawk in his *Autobiography*. "Yet instead of this *honorable course . . . I was forced into war*."

Atkinson laments having allowed the Militia to move ahead of the Army; the opportunity for peaceful resolution has disappeared.

Twelve militia and five Sauk are dead.

The winds keep whipping across the long-stretching fields as I head toward Dixon, thirty-two miles by car from Prophetstown. I am racing the clock because it has just now occurred to me how much territory I have to cover, and because I am not yet convinced that the weather will spare me. North winds rock the car on the eastbound roads. What little snow can still be lifted from the hardened ice-cover streams across the lanes.

Later, I read about another winter on the prairie, called the Winter of the Deep Snow. An account by Dr. Julian M. Sturtevant, who would soon become founder of Illinois College, reads:

> The clouds passed away and the wind came down from the northwest with extraordinary ferocity. For weeks, certainly for not less than two weeks, the mercury in the thermometer tube was not, on any one morning, higher than 12 degrees below zero. The wind was a steady, fierce gale from the northwest, day and night. The air was filled with flying snow, which blinded the eyes and almost stopped the breath of anyone who attempted to face it. No man could, for any considerable length of time, make his way on foot against it.

Sturtevant's account tells of the winter of 1830–31 on the Illinois prairie, a year before the Black Hawk War. Across the river, banished west of the Mississippi, their corn harvest destroyed by whites squatting at Saukenuk and supplies from the U.S. government too meager, the Sauk nearly starve in the winter of 1830–31.

Dixon, Illinois, takes its present-day fame as the Boyhood Home of Ronald Reagan. But today I'm chasing Black Hawk instead. I hope to see what I can find at the town's Historic Center at the old Dixon High School building on Reagan Way, the stately four-square brick building with the plaque that proclaims Reagan's attendance at the school in 1920. But no one answers the door.

So I'm on toward Stillman Valley, population 1,100. Established in 1875, more than forty years after the conclusion of the Black Hawk War, the town takes its name not from the historic rout but from Stillman Creek, which was named after Major Stillman (a fine distinction insisted upon in the town's literature). Along State Highway 72, past the gas station and the Valley Covenant Evangelical Church, lies a memorial cemetery for the twelve militia volunteers killed in Stillman's Run. Twelve plain, white-marbled headstones with names largely eroded, stretch out across the snow.

A monument erected in 1934 puts it bluntly:

> Here, on May 14, 1832, the first engagement of the Black Hawk War took place when 275 Illinois militiamen under Major Isaiah Stillman were put to flight by Black Hawk and his warriors. So thoroughly demoralized were the volunteers that a new army had to be called into the field.

Another face of the monument raises the ante, introducing a soldier who played a minor role in the war: "The presence of the soldier, statesman, martyr, Abraham Lincoln, assisting in the burial of the honored dead, has made this spot more sacred."

———————————

The "war" had few actual full-fledged battles between the legion of U.S. soldiers and Sauk. But outlying skirmishes, raids, and ambushes filled in the gaps while the Sauk women, children, and elderly were encamped far away. Many involved tribes other than the Sauk. A partial list of skirmishes includes:

• Saturday, May 19: Six soldiers are attacked by a Sauk warrior party about twenty miles from Stillman's Run. One soldier is killed;

- Monday, May 21: In what becomes known as the Indian Creek Massacre, fifty Potawatomie and three Sauk kill fifteen settlers. Two teenage girls, Sylvia and Rachel Hall, are taken captive. The Sauk claim they took the girls captive to save their lives from the Potawatomie. The girls are turned over to the Winnebago, who return them to the Whites. The rampage and abduction becomes a rallying cry against the Sauk.

- Thursday, May 24: A band of thirty Winnebago sympathetic to the Sauk kill four men sent by General Atkinson to carry messages to Galena, Illinois, and on to Fort Armstrong.

- Wednesday, June 6: Two Volunteers are ambushed—one killed—by a small group of Winnebago near Blue Mound, Wisconsin. The incidents have crept northward.

- Thursday, June 14: Six Volunteers, taking temporary leave to hoe corn in a field near the Pecatonica River, are attacked by Kickapoo warriors. Four are killed.

- Saturday, June 16: Seventeen Kickapoo warriors kill Henry Apel near the Pecatonica River.

- Sunday, June 24: One hundred and fifty Sauk warriors attack settlers at the Apple River Fort. Mrs. Elizabeth Armstrong gains historic fame—and the eventual naming of the town, Elizabeth, Illinois—when she organizes the women into squads to mold bullets and reload guns. The battle lasts forty-five minutes, with one settler dead and one wounded.

Amateur historians have no grounds to "speculate," I warn myself. But I can't avoid it, and this pursuit was never meant to be a history in the first place. I've been meaning to tell a landscape, and history keeps gumming up the works.

I can't avoid speculating how much Black Hawk must have loved the Rock River. Already my modern-day route has crossed and re-crossed the Rock River at least seven times as I pass into Wisconsin, and much of the pathway has paralleled the river. As Black Hawk's band forged deeper northeast, perhaps he followed the Rock River because it offered easy passage and, of course, a steady supply of water and decent food replenishment. But that alone doesn't explain it for me. An escape plan usually includes minimizing your pursuants' knowledge of where you are, and a riverine path is quite predictable.

I've got to think that he loved this river. The Rock River had bathed his native Saukenuk, and he had undoubtedly paddled it frequently in his travels that had taken him to Illinois, Wisconsin, and even partway on his visits to the British in Canada in his earlier years. Now on the run, perhaps he was soothed by the familiar waters.

Today as I travel, the Rock River is frozen beneath another Winter of the Deep Snow. The highway parallels it, crosses it, entwines with the river. Woodlands shape the riverbanks in the snowfall; empty docks and piers promise summer's fun.

Crossing over from Illinois into Wisconsin, I settle on Fort Atkinson as my first night's rest. I've worked my way back into the pathway of the snowstorm from earlier in the week. As the sun dips below the western horizon, I sluice through the barely cleared streets, find myself a room at a local hotel chain (where, unfortunately, the pool is closed for repairs), and head downtown for dinner.

Dinner at the Black Hawk Tavern, original location of the Black Hawk Hotel, established in 1848. A few blocks from the Rock River.

Of course.

President Andrew Jackson, outraged at the slow resolution of the Black Hawk War and the humiliating defeat of Stillman (reported widely in the Press), fires General Atkinson on June 15, ordering Major General Winfield Scott to replace him and to bring along a fresh force of troops from the East. However, the new recruits bog down in Detroit with a deadly epidemic and do not arrive before the war's end. The fired Atkinson continues leading the troops in the absence of his replacement.

On July 1, Black Hawk breaks the Sauk camp at the swamps surrounding Lake Koshkonong near present-day Fort Atkinson, and continues north up the Rock River.

On July 5, General Atkinson arrives at the swamps of Lake Koshkonong.

On July 6, General Dodge arrives at Atkinson's camp with his militia force of Volunteers.

————————

On the second morning, I awake to find a fresh dusting of snow on the car. Having wandered back into the brunt of the snowstorm, my immediate plan is to check the condition of the roads heading north. If necessary, I'll have to head back home to the west bank of the Mississippi, to Dubuque, and resume the trek when the roads have cleared. I email back home to say I'll decide in a few hours whether to continue.

But the sun is bright and the highways cleared. The wind chill is still sub-zero, and already there are occasional spots on the road where the wind is pushing trace amounts of loose snow across the clearing, but I'll wait and see whether that will be a problem later in the day.

State Highway 26 will take me through the towns of Jefferson, Johnson Creek, and Watertown, en route to Horicon Marsh—or Cranberry Lake—Black Hawk's most northerly campsite. Along the way I'll cross the Rock River at least four more times.

————————

A hand-lettered sign painted on a faded slab of plywood just outside of Jefferson, population 6,000, reads: "No Wal-Mart."

At the edge of town, the new Wal-Mart nears completion.

There is always a new glacial march underway.

————————

On July 18, Black Hawk and the Sauk encamped at Cranberry Lake are weary, hot (the temperature the day before having reached

86 degrees), and low on food and supplies. It is time to give up the fight, time to get the women and children back west of the Mississippi. They break camp and head south for twenty miles before turning west near present-day Watertown.

On July 18, Dodge's men arrive at Lake Sinissippi and pitch their tents at the rapids where the Rock River exits. Three local Winnebago report that Black Hawk and his band had rested here but are now at Cranberry Lake, just eight miles north.

———————————

Turning off Highway 26 onto County Road 60, I roll toward Hustisford, Wisconsin, on Lake Sinissippi, population 1,135. The terrain has again begun to change. Now the still-prevalent flatlands are punctuated with long, north-south finger-like hills, undoubtedly glacial drumlins laid down by the scouring and melting patterns of the last continental glacier.

In the valley lies the glacial-sculpted lake. The world consists of three distinct colors on this late morning: the pale blue of the bright, clear, winter sky; the brown of tree trunks, bushes, and homes; and the white of the snow piled high along the roadsides, on the streets (unsalted, unmelted), as well as the large white expanse stretching unbroken across the lake, except where, here and there, small scars have been plowed through for ice-fishing.

I could like this.

When the noon whistle blows, I scout out Diane's Bar and Grill, and order the Basic Burger with a Diet Coke. Later I ask two men at the bar—one younger than me, one pushing seventy—if they knew where Koch's Mill was located. Koch's Mill once sat at the rapids, where Dodge had camped, a prospect that excited me in the curious way that those of us not named Smith find it vaguely interesting to see our family name pop up far away from home.

"There's a marker at the park by the river," one of the men suggests.

The marker makes no reference to Koch's Mill, but to a sawmill once run by John Hustis, who founded the town at the site of the former Winnebago village in 1837. The difference, I assume, is simply another slippage in the knots of time.

This, then, was the campsite of Dodge's Volunteers on July 18 and Black Hawk just the week before.

I have scented the trail.

I have to get to Horicon Marsh before the scent goes cold.

Dodge prepares to head north to Cranberry Lake. He sends two Volunteers and a Winnebago guide, Little Thunder, south to Atkinson's camp at Fort Koshkonong to deliver the news that Black Hawk is encamped there. Before the messengers reach Atkinson, however, they find the trail of Black Hawk fleeing west just seven miles south of Lake Sinissippi. They return, instead, to Dodge with the news.

The trail is fresh! No need to go north when the enemy's already come back down south!

On the morning of July 19, Dodge's men break camp, head west, and pick up the trail after a scant twelve miles.

I'd visited Horicon Marsh once before. I'd gone there with my wife and kids, in October, when you're supposed to, and we were duly rewarded with a view of migrating ducks, geese, and other waterfowl, gathering and eating and splashing and making a general merry ruckus just prior to their long migration.

The 32,000-acre marsh—21,000 acres of which is a national wildlife refuge—harbors half a million migrating waterfowl (especially Canadian geese) each fall, as well as being summer home to 290 bird species. In winter, hawks and bald eagles scour over the frozen swamps, on the prowl for rodents and other small mammals.

Today the wind is howling down from the north, the marsh frozen over, and the Visitors Center closed for renovations. You can't tell where the grassland ends and the marsh begins. In the raw wind, I read the signboards about the glaciers and waterfowl migration. I walk on the ice crust back to the snow-packed parking lot.

No one I ask in town knows the location of Black Hawk's camp. At the library I find a book explaining a "legend" that Black Hawk had hid in an oak tree where Hubbard Street now crosses the railroad tracks while U.S. army scouts slept at its base. A thrilling story, but highly unlikely. Did the scouts simply not see the other 1,499 Sauk?

Even so I photograph the Hubbard Street sign. And the railroad crossing.

And then I head south and west on the highway. For Black Hawk is racing to the Mississippi with General Dodge in pursuit.

During our encampment at the Four Lakes, we were hard put to, to obtain enough to eat to support nature. Situate in a swampy, marshy country, (which had been selected in consequence of the great difficulty required to gain access thereto,) there was but little game of any sort to be found—and fish were equally scarce.... We were forced to dig roots and bark trees, to obtain something to satisfy hunger and keep us alive! Several of our old people became so much reduced, as actually to die with hunger! And finding that the army had commenced moving, and fearing that they might come upon and surround our encampment, I concluded to remove my women and children across the Mississippi, that they might return to the Sac nation again. Accordingly, on the next day, we commenced moving, with five Winnebagoes acting as our guides, intending to descend the Ouisconsin.

—Black Hawk, *An Autobiography*,
as he passes through the Four Lakes region,
including the isthmus separating Lake Mendota
and Lake Monona in present-day Madison,
Wisconsin.

Deep swamps and sink-holes were met by the army, nearly the entire distance. The men had frequently to dismount and wade in water and mud to the armpits, while the first night out a

violent thunderstorm with phenomenal rainfall, followed by an
unseasonable drop in the temperature, increased the natural dif-
ficulties of the march.

—Reuben Gold Thwaites, describing the
Volunteers' chase from Hustisford to Wisconsin
Heights, through the Four Lakes region.

———————————

To best follow the route of Black Hawk and Dodge after Horicon
Marsh, I ought to head south toward Rock Lake, near Mills, Wisconsin, then shoot west to the Four Lakes, pass between Lake Mendota
and Monona in Madison, and then swing northwest to cross the
Wisconsin River at a place called Wisconsin Heights, near present-
day Sauk City.

But that route would put me in Madison at rush hour, and trying
to find the exact location where Black Hawk had passed would mean
having to compete for a parking space in the snow-heaped city, and
walking in sub-zero wind chills to the hallowed spot, dodging the
traffic zipping by.

Or I could, to use John Wayne lingo, try to head them off at the
pass by driving directly to Sauk City and hunkering down for the night.

Reconnaissance is everything. I cell-phone home to my wife as I
hit the highway with changed plans: Please check Sauk City hotels on
the internet for me, and see what you can find.

The snow is the deepest yet as I drive into town just a half-hour
before sunset. My wife has located the Cedarberry Inn.

The pool is wonderful.

———————————

For three days the Militia Volunteers pursue the trail as quickly
as they can, through the marshes at the Four Lakes, to the bluffs approaching Wisconsin Heights, always a day or two behind, but gaining. The trail marks they encounter suggest the Sauk travel like geese
in flight, in a wedge, with one main central path and two side tracks.
There are signs the Sauk are starving, stripping trees back and digging for roots and tubers to eat.

The land is growing more rugged. Lieutenant James J. Justice fears that the Sauk are drawing them into the wild forests: "From the top of one stupiendous hill we could view nothing but the savage wilds of high hills and narrow Vales."[6]

Early on Saturday, July 21, a surgeon for the Volunteers returns from the advance guard saying that he has seen, killed, and scalped a Sauk. Three more ailing Sauk—unable to keep up with the desperately fleeing band—are discovered, two killed. The surgeon gets himself another scalp.

About 6 p.m. the Volunteers spy the rear guard of the Sauk, who quickly make ready for what will become known as the Battle of Wisconsin Heights. But the battle itself is a diversionary tactic, a delaying device meant to give women, children, and the elderly time to get across the Wisconsin River, in the westward trek toward the Mississippi.

The battle lasts for an hour, the Volunteers entrenched on the northern bluff, the Sauk warriors on the southern, Black Hawk shouting directions to his men from a white horse on the tallest hill. Only one Volunteer is killed. Dodge speculates at least forty Sauk killed, although Black Hawk reports only six.

By 7 p.m. the Sauk warriors are disappearing into the neighboring woods, and by nightfall most have crossed the Wisconsin.

The next morning Black Hawk and the Sauk are nowhere to be found, and the Volunteers, low on provisions, make a diversionary thirty mile march to Blue Mounds Fort on July 23, resuming the chase with Atkinson's Army Regulars four days later.

After all their [militiamen's] boasting, the simple fact was, that Black Hawk, although encumbered with the women, children, and baggage of his whole band, covering himself by a small party, had accomplished the most difficult of military operations, —to wit, the passage of a river, —in the presence of three

---

6.   As reported in *Black Hawk: The Battle for the Heart of America*, by Kerry A. Trask.

regiments of American volunteers! And they were now gone
—the victors could not tell us whither.

> —U.S. cavalry officer Philip St. George Cooke,
> recounting from Blue Mounds Fort the militia-
> men's boasting of their "victory" at Wisconsin
> Heights, 1832

———————————

In this skirmish with fifty braves, I defended and accomplished
my passage over the Wisconsin. . . . I would not have fought
there, but to gain time for my women and children to cross to an
island.

> —Black Hawk, *An Autobiography*

———————————

The temperature has eased slightly overnight, rising into the low
20s. When I pull out of the hotel parking lot en route to Wisconsin
Heights just five miles south of Sauk City, the icy snow still lies thick
on the trees, the mist heavy on the Wisconsin River. The tree trunks
rise out of the snow like brown soil siphoned up through straws, then
divide into branches, limbs, and twigs that change imperceptibly over
to a frost-encrusted white. Every tip of every tree is white.

There has been no ugly snowmelt yet. Now five days beyond the
brunt of the snowstorm, the street sides are still white, and the tire
tracks on the road have just barely scraped the pavement.

At Wisconsin Heights, I park the car and put on snowpants and
snowshoes, and head up into the hillside. The site is now a DNR
wildlife refuge. Back in the Driftless Land, the landscape has changed
again, with one hill competing with the next for towering rights.

My snowshoes make a stomping path up the hillside. It is hard to
keep my quest in mind as I begin, hard to think about Black Hawk
passing this way in desperation, Dodge in determined anger. The
woods couldn't hold any more beauty. This heavy, wet snow still
clumps in the crotches and branches of the trees and weighs down
the smallish bushes.

My first diversion from the path is to the Native American burial mounds near the top of the bluff. These burial mounds—long, linear mounds stretching out 70 feet along the snow—predate the Black Hawk War, have no association with the War whatsoever, except by way of providing some locational irony in their proximity to the battle site.

Soon, however, the path takes me to the battlefield itself. To the north, the hills from which Dodge's men shot across the ravine. To the south, the bluff where Black Hawk's warriors fought back. To the west, where women, children, and the elderly hurried across the Wisconsin River.

Myself and band having no means to descend the Ouisconsin, I started, over a rugged country, to go to the Mississippi, intending to cross it, and return to my nation. Many of our people were compelled to go on foot, for want of horses, which, in consequence of their having had nothing to eat for a long time, caused our march to be very slow. At length we arrived at the Mississippi, having lost some of our old men and little children, who perished on the way with hunger.

—Black Hawk, *An Autobiography*

Even U. S. Highway 14 still has scattered snow- and ice-packed sections as I head west toward the Mississippi. A mile of open road might be followed by a random patch of ice, so I have to take it easy. Even more so as I turn off onto State Highway 56, for the final leg to the place where I'll reach the Mississippi at Genoa and turn south toward the town of Victory and slightly beyond to Bad Axe River.

But I don't mind the slower pace, especially on Highway 56. For miles the road takes a general descent toward the Mississippi, through hills and bluffs that cut and slice in odd and random angles.

Three kinds of brown are etched against a deep white: standing woods of oak, hickory, maple, and scrub trees; limestone outcroppings where the earth's solid bedrock pokes through like bone piercing the skin; and the downed trunks of dead and decaying trees. In winter I am always amazed at how the dead seem to rival the living among the trees in the forest. In summer the dead fall away, subsumed in the understory growth of weeds and vines.

These are the hills I imagine the Sauk hurrying through, in summer heat, aiding a compatriot, then reluctantly acquiescing to another's plea to leave him behind for the good of the clan. These are the hills I imagine the Volunteers hurrying through in summer heat, outraged over the summer's events, wanting to get this war over, wanting life to return to normal, wanting to get to new farmlands in Illinois and Wisconsin promised them by the U.S. Government.

Finally, the Mississippi River.

Eight days after the Battle of Wisconsin Heights, on July 29, the Army and Militia Volunteers pick up the trail again, stumbling first upon an abandoned camp, and then, thereafter, upon scenes of starvation and desperation:

> *I witnessed scenes of distress and misery exceeding any I ever*
> *expected to see in our happy land. Dead bodies, males &*
> *females, strewed along the road—left unburied exposed—poor—*
> *emaciated beings—some dead from wounds recd. [received]*
> *in the engagement on the Ouisconsin—others by disease. The*
> *elms—the limbs along their routes were barked to give them*
> *food. Scattered along the route lay vestiges of [horses] tired out*
> *by travel—and killed to give life & sustenance to their master.*
> —Army Lieutenant Robert Anderson

The chase intensifies, the distance between pursuant and pursued narrowing by the hour. By evening on Wednesday, August 1, the Militia comes upon the smoldering fires of Black Hawk's camp, just abandoned that morning.

On August 1, Black Hawk and the remainder of his band reach the eastern shore of the Mississippi, just south of the Bad Axe River, thirty miles south of present-day La Crosse, Wisconsin. Some have died of starvation, some have been killed in battle, and some have taken an alternative route down the Wisconsin River to get to the Mississippi. Less than a thousand are with him this morning, gazing at the river, marveling at their good luck in escaping the Volunteers, taking in a breath before crossing the river to safety.

We had been here but a little while, before we saw a steam boat (the "Warrior") coming. I told my braves not to shoot, as I intended going on board, so that we might save our women and children. I knew the captain, and was determined to give myself up to him. I then sent for my white flag....The people on the boat asked whether we were Sacs or Winnebagoes. I told a Winnebago to tell them we were Sacs, and wanted to give ourselves up! A Winnebago on the boat called to us to "run and hide, that the whites were going to shoot!"

—Black Hawk, *An Autobiography*

The beginning of a bad end is underway by 4 p.m. when the steamboat *Warrior*, chartered from Prairie du Chien by Army Captain Gustavus Loomis, is returning from an upstream visit to elicit the cooperation of the Sioux on the western shores of the river. Cannon and musketfire rake the Sauk on the eastern shore. Twenty-five Sauk are killed.

By 6 p.m. the steamer ends its volleys and heads back south to Prairie du Chien and a good night's sleep.

Near sunset, Black Hawk himself unveils his plan to abandon the Sauk, taking with him the Prophet, both of their families, and a small contingent of about twenty-five warriors, arguing that by doing so he can draw the Militia northward and give the Sauk time to cross the Mississippi. But no one is buying the ploy. One Sauk, Wee-sheet, later will say, "Now they have brought us to ruin and lost us our women and children, they have to save their own lives." In the morning Black

Hawk regrets his actions and returns to the edge of the battle, acting
as a rear guard. But he doesn't enter the fray, and later escapes.

At 2 a.m., August 2, General Atkinson's men start stirring,
Dodge's and General James Henry's a little later. They are closing in
on the chase. A diversionary force of Sauk draws Atkinson's Regulars
away from the main body, but the Militia arrive full force by 9 a.m.
The fighting erupts into a frenzy, with Sauk panicking to get to the
water, women and children being fired upon as they rise up out of the
grass:

> *The men had marched a great way, through swamps, over*
> *mountains, and through the worst kind of forest . . . in order*
> *that they might have it in their power to assist in expelling from*
> *their country, those wretched children of the forest.*
> —John A. Wakefield, surgeon, Illinois Militia

> *At length, after descending a bluff, almost perpendicular, we*
> *entered a bottom thickly and heavily wooded, covered also with*
> *much underbrush and fallen timber, and overgrown with rank*
> *weeds and grass; plunged through a bayou of stagnant water,*
> *our men as usual holding up their arms and cartridge boxes. A*
> *moment after, we heard the yells of the enemy; closed with them,*
> *and the action commenced.*
> —*Military and Naval Magazine*, 1833

> *Our braves, but few in number, finding that the enemy paid no*
> *regard to age or sex, and seeing that they were murdering help-*
> *less women and little children, determined to fight until they*
> *were killed.*
> —Black Hawk (in absentia), *An Autobiography*

> *Many of the men, women and children fled to the river and en-*
> *deavored to escape by swimming. . . . Our troops arrived on*
> *the bank and threw in a heavy fire which killed great numbers,*

unfortunately some women and children, which was much de-plored by the soldiers.

—Lt. Albert Sidney Johnson

At 10 a.m., the *Warrior* makes another sudden appearance coming up from Prairie du Chien, raking the river bank with cannon and rifle fire, then turning its guns on the Sauk attempting to swim the river, including women with children on their backs. The river runs red, floats bodies for days.

Those who make it across have yet another surprise in store. The *Warrior*'s visit to the west-bank Sioux the previous day had enlisted their help in rounding up and killing off the escaping Sauk, a task the Sioux eagerly embrace against a common enemy.

The safety of the Iowa shore brings 150 Sioux down against the bloody, wet, and weary Sauk.

Around noontime, I turn south onto Wisconsin Highway 35, emerging from the bluffs and highlands and emptying myself at river level. Thick winter clouds now dull the river and the bluffs, and make the sky disappear. Soon the highway reveals the town of Victory, Wisconsin, founded in 1852 and named unabashedly for the Army/Militia's final rout of Black Hawk's band. Today the green road sign proclaiming the town of Victory is chipped and pocked with rust, and the town, nestled in the bluff side, suffers from typical small-town decay.

But nothing hides the sharp inverted V-shaped Battle Bluff just south of the Bad Axe River, where I pull off the road to read the historical markers I have seen several times before:

Battle Bluff ←Elevation 1139 ft.

Battle Hollow → Severe fighting one mile east between General Henry's 300 Il. militia and 300 Sac Indians, Aug 2, 1832.

Battle Island ← Hard fighting opposite. 1200 white soldiers engaged, 17 killed, 12 wounded. Of Indians, 150 shot, 15 drowned, 50 taken prisoners. 300 crossed river of whom 150 were killed by Sioux instigated by Gen. Atkinson. Of the 1,000 Sacs who crossed the river in April 1832, "not more than 150 survived to tell the tragic story of the Black Hawk War."

I put on my snowshoes to wander the valley a bit to get a feel for the lay of the land, but abandon the walk quite shortly. The point seems to be lacking.

After a while, I cross the highway and enter Blackhawk Park, an Army Corps of Engineers camping and recreation area on the site of the massacre. A park road winds over a mile amid the backwaters before ending at a boat launching loop. There, another marker announces Black Hawk's attempt to surrender on the previous evening and the *Warrior*'s engagement of fire, "killing 23 Indians suing for peace."

Within a few days, Black Hawk surrendered himself to the Winnebago, who brought him to the U.S. authorities. The Sauk and Mesquakie were forced to cede more than thirty thousand additional square miles of land west of the Mississippi—including the location of my hometown, Dubuque, where miners quickly flocked to scoop lead out of the ground.

Black Hawk himself would be paraded about the eastern United States as the "captured savage" before being released to Sauk lands in southern Iowa.

I'm feeling a bit wrung-out. How can I even think that I've traced Black Hawk's trail when I've zipped along highways at 60 miles per hour in a car, warm and comfortable in the below-zero wind chills? Danger for me has meant not making stupid decisions about road conditions.

But even so, I've been on the road, alone, chasing Black Hawk for three days and five hundred miles across ice-covered roads, and I *knew* it was going to come to this, I *knew* this is where it ended, and *how*. And yet I'm not prepared for the heaviness I feel.

The marker at the river bank tells two other stories. The first reveals that the same island where Black Hawk attempted to surrender before being fired on by the *Warrior* had also been used as a campsite of Zebulon Pike in 1805, months after his stop in Saukenuk.

The second story on the marker strikes a brighter note: "Here lived Nora Spaulding, who in Oct 1904 rode an unbroken colt to Victory at 2 a.m. and saved a limited train from going thru a burned culvert."

Life goes on.

At 2 p.m. on my third day of travel, I take one last glimpse of Battle Bluff, shut the car door, and begin the drive back home.

It was never my intent to write a war story. I've always been the kind to roll my eyes when Civil War aficionados give you a play-by-play of who took whom up what particular ridge, or when high school history teachers explained precisely how the Allied troops chiseled their advantage in World War II. I'm dangerously close to being able to tell you this about the Black Hawk War.

But I keep coming back to this:

The hills and bluffs that I love along the Mississippi River—the places where I hike and ski, and bicycle, and drive, and admire—have been loved and desired and regarded as sacred by others, too. It's long been established that the land can be bought for cash, but its more dear purchase and loss is by heart and soul and blood.

Maquoketa Caves:
The Landscape Beneath

The Dancehall cave was still closed for the winter when I snowshoed through the park in the middle of March.

I'd wandered the Maquoketa Caves many times over the years in the warmer seasons—ducked my way through the lighted Upper Dancehall and blinked in the sudden spray of sunlight where the underground trail emerges at the massive Middle Dancehall rock shelter. I'd shimmied through Fat Man's Misery and wondered if a good, solid shove would put an end to the seventeen-ton Balanced Rock. I'd let my kids do the exploring through the smaller caves that require crawling and grappling, and at last count they'd all come back out.

But now there was a foot of snow on the ground in a year with a relentless winter grip, and somewhere between Five hundred to nine hundred Big Brown Bats were still hibernating in the underground passages, so the caves were off-limits. Quite all right. With my snowshoe crampons tenaciously gripping the ice-encrusted snow, I was more than eager to check out some back corners of the park often overlooked in the caving season.

Maquoketa Caves is a state park located in eastern Iowa's Jackson County. The park's sixteen caves—the most in any Iowa location—include the 1,100-foot paved and lighted winding passage through the Dancehall Cave for those of us who take our subterranean adventures watered down. Some of the other caves require crawling through clayish mud and presume an absence of claustrophobia. Needless to say, I have not been inside them.

Still, the Caves offer one of the best examples of bedrock geology of the upper Midwest. In these regions, limestone formed in shallow Silurian and Ordovician seas 400-500 million years ago when lime from decaying sea shells mixed with the gathering, compressed, sedimentary muck. When the land uplifted (and fell, and uplifted again, several times), the muck and lime compacted into thick limestone bedrock layers separated by thinner, wafer-like layers of muddy shale.

Unlike shale, limestone dissolves when bathed in a steady stream of underground acidic water over millions of years, as occurred long ago when the water table was higher than at present. Groundwater settled into cracks and holes, dissolving more limestone through the eons. When nearby rivers downcut to levels lower than the passageways, the water tables fell too, leaving behind the labyrinth of caves.

At Maquoketa Caves, the overlying roof to the central cave partially crumbled, creating a valley along the old cave floor, and leaving a natural bridge in a thin band where the ceiling remained intact. The exposed valley created horizontal entrances to what had been a system of side-caves.

As your elementary-school science teacher once taught you, water dripping ever so slowly from cave ceilings leaves behind tiny amounts of calcium carbonate that grow into snow-white formations drop by drop at an inch per century. Those hanging tight to the ceiling like icicles are stalactites. Those formed by drippings on the cave floor are called stalagmites. When they drip long enough to join top to bottom, they form a calcified column.

Maquoketa Caves, with its long access to the unsupervised public, no longer offers the best display of stalactites and stalagmites. For that, head to some of the area's commercial caves, like Crystal Lake Cave in Dubuque, Iowa, where you can gaze at cave flower, popcorn, flowstone, or drapery formations. Or Cave of the Mounds in Blue Mound, Wisconsin, where the underground passageways sprout hollowed-out stalactites called soda straws, or floor-dripping formations called lily pads. Or Spook Cave near McGregor, Iowa, where visitors take a small underground boat tour among the formations. The cave got its name from early settlers who'd heard strange noises gurgling up from an opening in the hillside.

My wife's childhood farm once sported a cave entrance that professional spelunkers explored when her grandfather bought the place in the 1930s. During her childhood, siltation eventually buried the cave entrance, and provided instead a farm pond and a skating rink in winter months. In my hometown, Dubuque, every ten years or so a city street or a neighbor's yard will disappear when an unknown cave (or long-abandoned lead-mine) roof gives out. Or . . . caves in.

Cave-ins in the countryside are called sinkholes. Caves near the surface may have a thin limestone roof, which itself may slowly dissolve until it collapses, and a small piece of farm field, meadow, or woods slumps into the hole. A sinkhole may be six feet in diameter, or may swallow a building.

Vertical caves may open at the lip of a rocky slope, providing habitat for snakes, bats, and other creatures. Toss in a stone to hear how long it clatters to the bottom. In winter, vertical caves may even breathe out their pockets of air that are warmer and lighter than the outside air. A handful of light, powdery snow will billow upward if you toss it across the opening.

This landscape of cave and sinkhole and limestone outcropping is known as a karst geological region. Our deep wells produce water rich in minerals leached down through the bedrock. But special care must be taken at the surface, as contaminated water can also quickly work its way through the underground passages to the drinking wells. Locally, we try to keep large livestock confinement operations at bay to guard against water contamination, but the state, beholden to corporate agriculture, relaxes the rules.

We go about our business not knowing or caring much what lies beneath the solid ground.

I am wandering, I realize, every bit as much as underground water wends along the cracks and fissures in the limestone. It is, I have told you, a late-winter day of awakening snow-melt at the Maquoketa

Caves, and I am snowshoeing across the natural bridge. I trounce through backwoods that will be thick with undergrowth in a few months. Later in the year, I would not find the see-through tree trunk with ice in the bottom of the trunk hole, and I would not hear the larger branches groaning in the wind or the clattering of the higher branches being knocked about at the tree-tops. I would not have found the toppled oak, whose upturned roots have unearthed chunks of limestone that may never before have seen the light of day. Later in the year I would have missed the snow drifts flowing down around the limestone outcroppings like small glaciers.

I turn back down into the valley, where the ice in the creek is old, yellow, and rotting. Collapsed ice slabs covered by a recent snow dusting betray deer and rabbit tracks. Sun-warmed boulders in the frozen creek have opened up the first few splashes of water around their base.

In the valley beneath the natural bridge, it is easy to see how the cave top collapsed. The smooth, eight-foot-tall rounded boulders in the valley were undoubtedly once part of the roof. Today, lying beside the creek, they are capped in ice and snow. The creek gurgles beneath the twelve-inch ice as it passes beneath the natural bridge. I step gingerly at first, but hearing no strain in the ice, I cross with quick confidence.

With the Dancehall Cave still closed, I climb the stairway built for access to the valley floor. The snow and ice have turned it more into a steep, slippery ramp than a stairway, but the snowshoe crampons dig in squarely.

We'll need some spring and summer weather before I can visit the caves themselves. Until then, they'll get along just fine without me as I go about my winter's business.

Dark and silent, these caves echo the mind made numb by winter, with miles of wandering passageways beneath the conscious world.

Spring Here

But this was the day of the year when spring became truly credible. Freezing night, but cold bright morning, and a brave, bright shining of sun that is new, and an awakening in all the land, as if the earth were aware of its capacities.

—Thomas Merton, *Learning to Love*

The ancients were on to something when they began the new year in March, to mark the beginning of spring. I might have tied New Year's Day directly to the Spring Equinox.

Better yet, I'd tie the New Year to whatever morning in spring we step outside, sniff the warming air, and collectively agree that, yes, the tide has turned. This would, of course, drive the calendar-makers wild, as every town would have its own New Year's Day. But such would mark at least the beginning of the psychological new year.

In that sense, the new year began last week around here, when the temperature found its way into the low 50s for the first time, the sun burnt through the cloud cover that is winter's most depressing feature, and the remnant snowbanks hissed and melted like doused witches. More importantly, I marked the beginning of spring—of the new year—with my first bicycle ride, the first eight miles en route, I hope, to at least three thousand more.

Several weeks ago I spotted the first returning V-formation of geese arising from the Mississippi, honking as they ascended the river bluffs at a height just barely clearing the rooftops. My wife spotted our first robin. The geese and robins are, I'm afraid, more optimistic than me, as early spring is an up-and-down affair. Tomorrow the temperatures will plunge again. There is a serious chance that we will still break the annual snowfall record with four more inches.

Still, we've talked of the new bushes we'll plant along the driveway and the house projects to be undertaken. We've talked about new creeks, rivers, and put-ins for canoeing, dates and destinations for family camping as spring unfolds into summer. I secretly guard the remaining days for bicycling.

But early spring is long and sometimes painfully inclement. I've put away the cross-county skis and snowshoes, but the woods are presently too muddy for hiking. Soon the rains will come and wash away winter dirt and salt. But one of these rains will be warmer. The worms will crawl out of their winter burrows.

Then, on the very next morning, when the sky clears and the sun speaks a new warmth, everything that is to be green will pop. It will be a new color, not seen since November. The lawn will turn first. Rhubarb will poke from the side garden. I'll plant a few tomatoes and green peppers. In the woods, the great, massive oaks will look a bit silly with first buds of baby green leaves. When, a few weeks later, the cherry tree in my front yard pushes out its white flower buds, I'll estimate my upcoming wealth of sour cherries, which no one else in my family eats.

I've seen this show before, I know how the storyline goes.

Still, we line up yet one more time to watch, amazed after all these years that the whole thing works, and doesn't require our oversight and design.

Just yesterday, a late-March snow put us over the top for the snowiest season on record, the progress having started in late November, while still officially autumn. This morning I walked on the golf course, snapping photos of the white-encrusted oaks against a brilliant blue sky. I don't quite have it in me to complain. But my bike stands ready in the basement, awaiting the final thaw.

It's proverbially true that April showers bring May flowers, but this year it also brought flooding. With eight inches of precipitation in April—including a late-season snow squall early in the month—the Mississippi and tributaries have swollen. Since 1968, Dubuque has kept the river at bay, protected by a floodwall and earthen dike. Unfortunately, the flood protection also kept the townspeople away from the river until the recent construction of walking and bicycling paths on top of the dike. On several occasions this spring I've been down to the river to watch the muddy, roiling froth whisk past the shoreline on serious business.

This spring's regional flooding is serious but not disastrous. (The disastrous Midwest flooding of 2008 would come in a second deluge, in early summer.) The Mississippi crested at 20.29 feet in Dubuque, about 3 feet over traditional flood stage. This is the highest it's been in a number of years, but it's nowhere close to the record-breaking 1965 crest of 26.9 feet that submerged the downtown and sent the city leaders scurrying to build the floodwall.

But my friends who enjoy river life on the unprotected backwater of Frentress Lake have opened up their basement doors to the Mississippi. Better to let a catfish explore the downstairs than to try locking out the ever-curious river. The latter will only result in the river beating down your basement doors and perhaps your foundation.

Farm fields are choked with water. Those in the flood plains of tributary creeks and rivers are—well—flooded, but even fields on higher ground are cloddy and muddy. My brothers-in-law—three bachelor-Irish farmers—wonder, as April rolls into May with no reprieve, how soon they can get planting or whether they will need to turn to short-season corn seed.

I meet one man, however, who relishes the high water. Jon Stravers of McGregor, Iowa, conducts bird inventories along the Mississippi for the Audubon Society and other organizations, and I hook up with him to take a flatboat excursion through the submerged backwater forests, scouting bald eagle and red-shouldered hawk nests. As we bump from tree to tree, he explains how high water brings him up close and personal to the nests he is checking. He can spend all day in a backwater cove "listening to the conversation" of hawks, neo-tropical birds just arrived to nest and rear their young, and, of course, the incessant honking of geese.

Living high on a hill, I am simply happy that my basement is dry.

Spring may stoke the fires of young love, but for prairie lovers spring means stoking prescribed prairie fires. Prairies need fire to remain healthy and to thwart encroaching woodlands, especially in a temperate climate like the Driftless. Before the arrival of European-Americans, prairie fires occurred naturally through lightning strikes or were set intentionally by Native Americans, who knew that, in the aftermath, the resurgent succulent grasses would draw bison and other game. European-Americans, however, plowed the prairie into farmland and fought fire with a vengeance, so that the occasional prairie remnant left to its own devices was slowly choked by spreading brambles, bushes, and trees.

Prescribed burns knock back the intruders long enough for prairie grasses and flowers to get a fresh start. Today at the Mines of Spain, my friend Dana is helping set fire in a flatland meadow, dripping a lighted diesel mixture from a fuel canister onto last year's dried-out grasses in long, whirly-cued lines, nursing it and coaxing it across the valley. Later he and Mines of Spain Park Ranger Wayne Buchholtz, along with an Americorps volunteer crew, will try to shoo the low-grade fire up into a wooded hillside. But the moist leaves and grasses aren't having much of it. A prescribed burn requires a lot of trained personnel and other volunteers, and so must be set up in advance, and this year the burn date has been preceded by wet weather. Overall, the burn turns out mildly successful, but not as thorough and penetrating as it might have been. It is wimpy enough that Dana even hands me the fire canister and says, "Here, try this."

Last spring I watched a burn at the Mines under just the right conditions. The flames raced through a prairie meadow, occasionally climbing to twenty-foot heights or more. Once the prairie floor was charred, the heat played tricks with air currents, spinning mini-cyclones of ash and dust, whirling like twisters across the field.

Spring was slow to arrive this year, after a record-snowfall winter that wouldn't loosen its grip. Even after the final thaw, unseasonably cold temperatures delayed the trees from sprouting, farmers from working their ground, and bicyclists from climbing their hills. The calendar was off by about a month.

Still, eventually everything sprouted and the bike came out of storage. The snow crab trees and cherry tree in my front yard set out their white flowers, the tulips bloomed, and I took my annual photographs that look just like last year's.

And now, too soon, spring is getting a little long in the tooth. The petals from the snow crabs and cherry are dropping like a new snow in the grass. In a week or so I'll check to make sure that the cherry flowers have been replaced by the green nubs of the future fruit. If they are, then I'll know that the storyline has played out just as it should, once again.

Mississippi Refuge

The word "river," back in its Latin roots, originally meant a shore, not the water itself. For word buffs, this explains a whole slew of shoreline words, like Riviera, riprap, and riparian. For river buffs, perhaps this shore-reference suggests that the real life of the river, as well as its saving graces, lies in the backwaters.

I arrived at the Mississippi River dock in McGregor, Iowa, at 9:45 a.m. (the word "arrive" originally meaning "to come to the shore") to meet Jon "Hawk" Stravers of the Audubon Society. He planned to spend this mid-April day on the backwaters, looking for red-shouldered hawk and bald eagle nests. My plan was to enjoy the river.

The water was high, though, just straddling flood-stage from recent rains and snowmelt. With a little trepidation, I called Jon just before leaving my home in Dubuque, an hour and a half downriver. "Is the water too high? If you think it would be better, we can reschedule for another day."

"You kidding?" he boomed over the phone. " It's my favorite season! I'll be out on the river today whether you're here or not." I was in my car within minutes. By 10 a.m. we were checking out our first eagle nest.

The Mississippi River carries as much meaning as it does water, and the meanings are as varied as its twisting shorelines. The river means flyway and nesting habitat for waterfowl, breeding habitat for fish and smorgasbord for fishermen, highway for barges, playground for skiers. For this canoeist and his wife, the Mississippi means a lazy summer afternoon's float.

The numbers are impressive. The Mississippi stretches, yawns, and meanders 2,300 miles from tiny Lake Itasca in northern Minnesota to its big, bold bathtub in the Gulf of Mexico. Along with its two most significant tributaries—the Missouri and the Ohio Rivers—it drains about 40 percent of the continental United States from the Rocky Mountains to western New York State. By the time it reaches the Gulf, it is pushing more than half a million cubic feet of water per second.

I could carry on about the Mississippi's power, strength, and size, but that isn't quite the story I want to tell. A quieter story—but perhaps the real story—floats in the backwaters, lingers on the edges. Particularly so on the Upper Mississippi River National Wildlife and Fish Refuge.

It requires some patience to sort through all the braids and backwaters of the story. There are competing and common interests among those who want to move grain on the river, fish the waters, ride their boats, or, like Jon Stravers, ensure good wildlife habitation. They are all part of the story.

_____

The Upper Mississippi Fish and Wildlife Refuge was established in 1924 at the urging of the Izaak Walton League in order to protect migratory waterfowl and fish habitat. Divided into four districts— Winona (MN), La Crosse (WI), McGregor (IA), and Savanna (IL)— the refuge spans 261 miles from Wabasha, Minnesota, to Rock Island, Illinois, and includes 240,000 acres of river, islands, backwaters, and shoreline. Although it comprises only 11 percent of the Mississippi's total river miles, the refuge boasts big numbers: 167 bald eagle nests and up to 2,700 bald eagles during spring migration; 50 percent of the world's canvasback ducks; 5,000 great blue herons and egrets; 119

fish species. Forty percent of the nation's waterfowl use the Mississippi, including the refuge, as their migration highway in spring and fall.

But unlike typical wildlife refuges that are self-contained, the Upper Mississippi Refuge shares its "place" with locks and dams operated by the Army Corps of Engineers, with private landowners, and with city-, county-, and state-owned lands stretching up and down the shoreline. And, according to Clyde Male, Assistant Manager of the McGregor District, the Congressional legislation that authorized the refuge also required that it not interfere with river commerce. As a result, he says, "Some things do occur on the river that are not consistent with conservation." For example, while the industry is quick to point out that barges transport grain, fuel, and other goods more efficiently than trucks and trains, conservationists argue that their huge propellers grind up the river bottom and churn up sediment, creating havoc for fish habitation. Regardless of the pros and cons, the enabling legislation prohibits the United States Fish and Wildlife Service (USFWS) from interfering with barge transportation.

Even dealing with the general public—especially boaters and fishermen—can be tricky on the Refuge. Some of the shore-hosting states have argued that the enabling legislation also means that the river—all of it—is open to boaters. But the USFWS maintains that the refuge's commitment to habitat protection allows certain sensitive backwaters to be kept off-limits to motor boats.

In making decisions about access, habitat restoration, boating regulations, and a host of other issues, the USFWS will typically have to work with some combination of the Army Corps of Engineers, neighboring states, hunters, fishermen, and conservationists. In addition, decisions have to be made through the lens of what is good for the immediate parcel of the refuge, what is good for the district, and what is consistent with the goals for the entire refuge and river.

It's a balancing act. When I talked with Clyde, he was looking forward to being out on the river the following day, doing wildlife counts.

Refuge: from Latin *refugium* < *re-* back + *fugere* – to flee + *ium*– place for. A place to flee back to.

"I am connected to the river from a spiritual basis to a work basis to a musical basis," Jon Stravers told me the first time I met him at a small upscale bar in Dubuque. He'd driven the hour and a half from McGregor to watch his friend coach a local high-school tennis team, and we took the opportunity to meet before heading out on the river the following week.

Stravers, a tall man with greying hair tied back in a smallish ponytail and a sun-and-wind tanned face already in April, explained that the Mississippi became his refuge when he returned from Vietnam in the 1970s. "My return strategy was to get in a canoe and escape," he said. The avocation soon became his vocation. He met Gladys Black, a self-taught ornithologist known as "Iowa's bird lady," who introduced him to the world of raptors and helped him get licensed for bird banding. Soon Jon was doing bird species surveys for the Audubon Society, the Fish and Wildlife Service, the Army Corps of Engineers, and area colleges, particularly specializing in red-shouldered hawks. For over twenty-five years, he's surveyed from Hastings, Minnesota, to Hannibal, Missouri, over a 500-mile stretch of river.

For several years, he essentially lived on the river for long stretches during the summers. From 2000-2005, he ran the Audubon Ark, an authentic paddle wheeler pushing a 40-foot barge, going from town to town along the Mississippi. He and his crew would deliver Audubon educational programs in each town, and host music fests that included Jon and whatever local talent came down to join him on the barge. Each summer they'd make three 30-day trips on the river. "It was pretty exciting, but almost too much. I'm used to time alone on the river, but with the Ark, there were always people around. Still, that's a big piece of river in your blood."

Jon's current raptor-survey work for the Audubon Society and other clients is more centered around the McGregor-Marquette area of the Mississippi. McGregor and Marquette are two small, neighboring northeast Iowa river towns of 871 and 476 people, respectively. The locale is also home to Effigy Mounds National Monument, a 2,500-acre historic and spiritual site that preserves over 200 Native American burial and ceremonial mounds—many of them in the shapes of birds and bears—built by the Hopewellian peoples 3,000 to 750 years ago. The river, raptors, bluffs, and the mounds themselves give him spiritual grounding. "In order to understand it all, I have to have a center that I go back to, and for me that is the area of the Effigy Mounds."

Jon's work also includes doing bird inventories for the DNR and helping with their forest stewardship plans in the blufflands along the river. "Twenty years ago, there were no conversations occurring between foresters and bird specialists. Now we're finally talking."

With a handshake, we made plans to head out onto the river together the following week.

——————————

The river's harnessing—if indeed it has been or can ever be harnessed—began in steps and stages. In the 1830s the U.S. government began clearing the river for commerce, hauling out snags, digging through sandbars, and even dynamiting rapids. By the 1870s they'd dug a 4.5-foot channel, and by 1907, constructed wing dams—long fingers of rock and boulders extending from the shore to force water to the center of the river where it swept out a more or less continuous six-foot channel.

But the twentieth century's diesel-powered tow barges required a nine-foot channel, and to accomplish this, the 1930s saw a massive WPA public works program to build twenty-nine locks and dams from St. Paul to St. Louis. The dams essentially keep the river in flat pools that descend in staircase fashion from one pool to the next downstream, and the locks act as elevators raising and lowering barges and other boats as they head north or south.

The natural river meandered and shifted in the flats between the tall bluffs that define its path through the Driftless Land—the bluffs themselves having been carved by the Mississippi when it coursed brim to brim with glacial meltwater twelve thousand years ago. Before the dams were built, water levels could vary greatly in the backwaters from year to year and season to season, a variation that actually kept the wetlands healthy by allowing vegetation to take hold in dry seasons.

The barge industry maintains that a single 15-barge tow hauls more cargo than two trains or 850 semi-trailers, and as such offers more fuel efficiency for commerce and the environment. At the same time, the dams that pool the river for barges cause siltation in the sloughs that harbor the best fish and wildlife habitat. Water moves more slowly through the pooled river, especially in the backwaters, and sediment from farm fields, excavation sites, and nearby towns settles out as the water slows. Plus, bottom sediment in the dam-flooded backwaters never dries out. Plants can't get their roots estab-lished in the fine, loose bottom. Finally, muddy water prevents sun-light penetration, further disabling plants.

The dams, of course, are not totally to blame for the siltation problem. In the natural environment, loosened sediments would be trapped and retained by grasses prior to entering the river system. "Now," says Clyde Male, "there is a direct line connection" from farm field runoff and parking lots to the streams and river.

The USFWS, in conjunction with the Army Corps of Engineers and state governments, is trying to improve the river through selec-tive habitat restoration projects on the Upper Mississippi Refuge. One such method is simply through the use of occasional "draw-downs," i.e., lowering a pool by controlling water releases at an up-stream dam. During a draw-down, the fringes of the backwaters will dry out, allowing plants to re-establish on the dried out shore. When the river level rises—due to rains or increase in the dam release, the new vegetation will thrive with its roots in the water, and provide a paddle-up-and-snack experience for ducks and other waterfowl.

The McGregor District of the refuge—Pools 9, 10, and 11 run-ning ninety-seven river miles from Genoa, Wisconsin, to Dubuque, Iowa—has in several locations built underwater structures or artifi-cial islands to divert flow into the main channel and away from the sloughs in an attempt to slow down siltation of the backwaters. And since siltation also wreaks havoc by smoothing out the river bottom, some restoration projects have involved dredging deep holes in the backwaters, especially where oxygen-rich streams enter the Mississippi. The dredged-out holes provide winter habitat, deep enough so they won't freeze solid and protected enough so that fish won't need to expend lots of winter energy fighting the river current.

Another project in the McGregor District involved creating an artificial rock island in a wide sweep of river to break up the wind and resultant waves that pummel and erode existing river islands. And the USFWS is getting its feet wet with a new type of project as it works to re-establish forest diversity in a section of upper Pool 9. The river bottomlands traditionally sported an assortment of American elm, swamp white oak, silver maple, and willow. But with the bottomlands more frequently flooded due to siltation, tree species other than the silver maple have been in decline. With backwater restoration and timber management, the USFWS hopes other species will rebound.

Such restoration projects are not a panacea, but they are helping. At the very least, says Male, they are "pushing the clock back fifty years. They 'mimic' rather than 'recreate' the old river."

Even so, Male considers the McGregor District, and Pool 9 in particular, to be the "crown jewel" of the upper Mississippi and indeed of the entire river's length. The lower Mississippi has a sister refuge called the Mark Twain National Wildlife Refuge, but it is more piecemeal than the continuous Upper Mississippi Refuge; as a result, the river is more diked and harnessed as it moves through the south, with less focus on habitat protection. "There is a wild nature to the river here despite the locks and dams that is not there in the lower Mississippi," says Male.

Even in the Upper Mississippi, the McGregor District is special, Male maintains. Farther south, there are fewer bluffs, meaning that farms and their inevitable runoff are located closer to the river. While the upper stretches of the river offer more marshes and wetlands, Male particularly likes the bluffs along the McGregor District, where he has served the USFWS since 1987. "Pool 9 is the most significant wildlife pool along the Mississippi," says Male. Using bald eagles as a measuring stick, the number drops off above and below Pool 9. There are fifty bald eagle nests on Pool 9 alone. Pools 8 and 9 are home to as much as two-thirds of the river's canvasback duck population of 800,000. And there are twenty thousand tundra (whistling) swans in this stretch of the river as well.

For wildlife, the river means refuge.

———————————

Waterfowl and raptors—and the river itself—are all making incredible comebacks due to habitat restoration, the ban on DDT, wildlife land acquisitions, and other environmental improvements, Jon Stravers said when I first met him. "I'm a creature of hope," he maintained. But even so, preserving large sections of river bottom and backwater is a continued necessity. "Unless you have five hundred acres of wild-ass woods, you won't have these hawks," he warned.

So on a Monday morning in mid-April, we are setting out on the river to check the neighborhood in Stravers' 18-foot flatbottom jonboat with the 50 h.p. Yamaha motor and "Audubon Mississippi River Program" sign taped to the steering deck. It is one of the first warm mornings in a slow-to-take-hold spring, one of the first where the sun works on the face and arms. When the boat revs up, however, a jacket still feels good against the breeze.

The river is hovering at flood stage, although it would need to rise several more feet to actually impair the town of McGregor. The last big flood had been in 2001, Jon recalls. The river was closed to traffic for twenty-seven days, although Jon had a permit to be on the water for his hawk surveys. "For twenty-seven days I only saw one other person on the river, so I like a good flood," he jokes, demonstrating his penchant for solitude.

Within minutes of the dock we cross mid-river into McGregor Lake to check on our first bald eagle nest, "just to say hello," but are surprised to find a goose has taken it over. But our main observation grounds lie downstream a couple of miles in the Sny Magill slough. We cut through water like glass en route to our second bald-eagle nest, where we spy the eagles circling above. The eagles lay their eggs in mid-March, and they hatch in mid-April. "Soon there will be young poking their heads out above the nest," Jon says.

Entering the backwaters in flood season allows us to boat right on up into the river-bottom woods. In surveying the red-shouldered hawk nests, Stravers returns to each site six times over a twelve-week period, and along the way he's interested in finding out what other birds are present. Today's task is to "listen to see who's showing up, who's talking." We hear a chickadee and a phoebe, as Jon points out their individual calls. The five-part song we hear is from the song sparrow. But most of the bird calls are being drowned out by a persistent goose ("Damn goose," Jon spits). Next up is the Yellow-bellied Sapsucker's hammering. As opposed to woodpeckers, the sapsucker hammers an irregular beat: "They're the percussionists that like to keep to a different rhythm."

In another backwater, Jon pulls out his flute and plays a call to see if he can get a response from a red-shouldered hawk. So far it's quiet.

In the lull, I ask Jon whether, most days, he knows where he's headed when he wakes up in the morning, or whether he decides at breakfast. He chuckles at the question. "Some of both! Sometimes the weather dictates the schedule." Some days are better for staying indoors and writing the reports. Sometimes he heads out the night before, either by boat or in his van, and sleeps in the van or on an island, so that he is on-site without disturbance at sunrise, and he can engage in his research even before he gets out of bed, just by listening. "You just wait in the right place and listen for the conversation." If all is well, there will be a certain intonation between the calls of the male and the female. If the nest is full, the male may have been up all night hunting for the female and the young. "When he brings something back, she responds in a certain way. If there are young in the nest, there is going to be conversation." But if something happens to the eggs, "There is not a conversation going on."

But Jon is not worried about the lack of a response call just yet. In mid-April the hawks are often still sitting on their eggs and may be quiet then.

Back on the river for a bit, we pull into shore at the Sny Magill Unit of the Effigy Mounds National Monument. The mounds that most people associate with the monument overlook the Mississippi from the impressive bluffs, but in this lesser-known unit, the mounds huddle almost at river level, at a small rise above the shore. Jon regards the mounds carefully: "As someone who lives here and feels spiritually connected to the land, I never fail to be affected by these mounds," he says. Lots of questions arise. "What were they doing, what was going on?" he asks. And why did they suddenly quit building the mounds a thousand years ago?

South of the mounds we spy another red-shouldered hawk nest, this time occupied. The female flies off as we settle into the slough. "Usually you can't sneak up on them," Jon explains. Once though, he startled a female in her nest when he approached from land. She had her back turned to Jon as she was feeding her young, tearing up bits of meat and parceling it out. When she discovered him near the tree, she swooped off the nest and dive-bombed, pulling up just short, then heaved herself up into the sky and dove again, sending Jon face-first into the mud where he felt the rush of wind from her wings.

Today's hawk, however, is content with some overhead reconnaissance.

Jon often locates a nest with relative ease, as the red-shouldered hawks like to settle in at a spot where a small spring-fed draw enters the river. There they will hunt small animals attracted to the stream. Hawks, Jon adds, have a "high nest-site fidelity." One nest he'd observed was active with the same pair of hawks for thirteen consecutive years. It was empty the fourteenth year, and then a new nest appeared in the same tree the following year. Jon speculates that perhaps one of the birds died and then the survivor re-mated.

Moving back upriver again, we slide past a couple dozen communal heron nests. They look comical with the large herons nearly toppling out of their undersized homes.

Across the river from Wisconsin's Wyalusing State Park, we spy a pair of eagles—Wyatt and Lucy—the female poking her head above the nest, the male perched like a sentry on a limb across the cut. They're a good pair, says Jon, who has seen this couple every year since 1991. He once saw Wyatt heft a muskrat back to the nest. Stopping for lunch in a backwater, we watch tree swallows, glimpsing the bit of iridescent blue on their backs. They like to nest in old woodpecker holes in dead tree trunks. Finally we hear the "kee-kee-kee" of a red-shouldered hawk, who keeps "saying the same thing over and over."

After lunch we push more deeply into the backwater and on into the flooded woodland. The motor, barely humming, bounces over a couple of floating logs until Jon cuts it entirely and propels us with the oars. "This might be a new one for you, huh?" he says as he picks a zig-zagging route among the trees and tells how he'd once—just once—gotten the boat wedged between two trunks. "Be prepared to be flexible," he tells me as we duck under low-lying branches and vines.

We row into a flooded woods where we watch a box turtle who doesn't seem frightened by our arrival. Turkey vultures circle overhead. Then Jon is looking for the prothonotary warbler, who should be showing up soon. They are neo-tropical birds that spend seven months in the tropics, come here to nest, and return to the tropics when the young are able to fly. "They break my heart every year when they leave," he says.

Stravers will spend every day from April through July out here on the river or in the surrounding blufflands, weather permitting. In winter he will walk the frozen backwaters, write, travel, visit family, "and sleep a lot." But here in spring, he will come to a flooded woods like this and spend most of the day. "Every sound in here means something," he says, explaining for example that a pileated woodpecker will pound differently for insects, courtship, and for territory. "For territory, they'll find the biggest, loudest tree in the forest."

Rowing through the flooded woods, Jon says, "People are attracted to the river in different ways. But when you can boat through the flooded forest, you don't run into a lot of people back here. This is my experience with the river. These few weeks in spring with high water, this is the part that got me thirty years ago. I will always be doing this as long as I'm physically able."

Finally we faintly hear two red-shouldered hawks. One adds an extra syllable: "kee-yaw, kee-yaw, kee-yaw." The extra syllable means it's a female, we're near the nest, and she doesn't like it. Although we haven't actually spotted the hawks or seen the nest, Jon says contentedly, "My work is done for the day. I know they're here."

It's a big, long river, the Mississippi. Probably everyone who loves the river will claim their own corner as their refuge. I don't claim to be a "river rat," as those who own boats, fish, or hang out on islands often call themselves. But a few years ago my wife and I bought a pair of canoes and headed out for the backwaters, where small motorless craft can avoid the wakes of barges and speeding pleasure boats.

We found our own refuge there.

In watching a heron take flight and land, take flight and land again as it sweeps an arc ahead of us, in listening to the yammering of birds on an island as we silently pass, in glimpsing the occasional bass break the glassy surface, we've learned, too, that the backwaters is where the action is. We've learned why the root of the word "river" points to its shore.

————————————

Jon Stravers has another visitor to take on the river this afternoon, and I have another appointment. When we clear the edge of the flooded forest, Jon revs up the motor and we press on back upriver, through the braided sloughs, through the channel, and arrive back at the McGregor dock at 2:30 p.m.

We've come to the shore.

Whitewater–Lost Canyon

The glacier lurked out there somewhere twenty thousand years ago, inching forward, retreating, advancing, gouging and grinding. It did not reach the Driftless Land, but its presence in the neighborhood exerted a chilling grip.

At the present-day site of Whitewater Canyon and Lost Canyon in northeast Iowa—more than one hundred miles removed from the ice mass in any direction—the nearby glacier's impact extended two hundred feet below ground.

Beneath the rolling hills of the prairie lay an alternative universe, an interlocking system of caves and underground waterways. Most of northeast Iowa exhibits a typical karst geology, with limestone bedrock laid down from sediment and the seashells of dying creatures from ancient Ordovician seas 450 million years ago. Limestone, however, is slowly dissolvable. When surface limestone dissolves from normal water seepage, soil collapses into the chasm, pock-marking the prairie with sinkholes, some of which may drain directly into the underworld. Deeper down, groundwater runs through the bedrock in streams, creating underground passages. When the water table dropped after the glaciers retreated, dried-up subterranean streambeds became caves.

And here we sit. The bedrock beneath us is not stable.

But at Whitewater and Lost Canyon, it was even less stable. For the roof was about to blow.

I arrived a few minutes late at the Whitewater Canyon parking lot, but that didn't seem to matter to Bob Walton. On this morning in early March given to rapid snowmelt, Bob had already spotted a red-winged blackbird on a fence post and a turkey vulture circling overhead. "Spring came last night!" Bob said, welcoming his first sightings of the season.

I'd been to the recently acquired Whitewater Canyon at the juncture of Dubuque, Jackson, and Jones Counties several times, but today, retired Dubuque County Conservation Director Bob Walton was going to show me a few sights and tell me a few stories beyond the trails. Walton was a key player in the acquisition of the 419-acre wildlife area which is about half grassland and half woodland, and most prominently features a cedar-draped 200-foot sheer canyon overlook of Whitewater Creek.

Whitewater Canyon had long been in the scope of conservationists. The Iowa DNR had been approached already in the 1950s about acquiring the land, but in the workaday thinking of the era, the DNR wasn't interested because the hills were too rugged to run a park road through. Without a road, picnic tables, pavilions, and swing sets, why on earth would anyone want to visit?

Times have changed, of course, and in this case for the better. The story of Whitewater's acquisition begins with Cliff and Jenny Waller. A land developer himself who'd turned a good profit selling property at the edge of Dubuque to Wal-Mart, Cliff decided to change paths and was on the lookout, according to Walton, "for the roughest, most undeveloped property in the county" as a private retreat. Jenny recalls Cliff bringing her the purchase papers in bed at four in the morning, saying, "Here, sign this!" She thought she was signing more legal documents from the Wal-Mart sale, but she never regretted the purchase of Whitewater Canyon. Cliff and Jenny owned the land for fifteen years. "Cliff and his buddies hunted there," says Jenny, "and we had some nice picnics. We'd go fishing, pick berries and mushrooms." One day near the end, Cliff had a slight stroke coming out of the property on his ATV and didn't quite remember where he'd been. "We decided that it was time to sell."

They soon began talking to Walton and the Dubuque County

Conservation Board with an offer to sell the land at a bargain price, so Whitewater Canyon could remain a wildlife haven. Developers would have loved to erect mansions on the overlooks, but Cliff "was adamant about not wanting to see houses on the property," says Walton.

Walton and other members of the Conservation Board quickly put together funding from an array of sources that blended hunting and non-hunting conservation and wildlife organizations, grants, and private donations. The fundraising moved at lightning speed despite assurances, says Walton, that Cliff "wouldn't sell the land out from under us."

You can almost feel the earth curving out from underneath you when you climb the gentle slope from the parking lot and emerge onto the grassland plateau. The horizons take in miles of rolling hills in every direction of the three counties. The drop-away hillsides harbor woodlands. The wind sweeps unobstructed, whether ushering in winter's northern gusts or today's first warm blush of spring air from the south.

The grass and woodlands offer habitat to over eighty-five species of nesting birds, more species counted than anywhere else in the county. The register includes worm-eating warblers, scarlet tanagers, Henslow's sparrows, and bobolinks. While any old habitat may be good for migrating birds, Walton says, "It takes someplace special to raise a brood."

Walton frequently paused, binoculars raised, to scope the horizon for turkey vultures and bald eagles. In the lingering snow he identified coyote, badger, deer, and bobcat tracks. He pointed out twenty grassland acres being converted to natural prairie by Pheasants Forever and the Audubon Society, and pointed to the rim of forest woodland with fingerling ridges extending out into the grasslands. "Edges are particularly important places of habitat," he explained, and the irregular shape of the forest-grassland juncture—nearly twelve miles of edge—make this habitat particularly rich.

But the best was yet to come as we veered off the curving trail and headed straight into forest, crunching through the crusted, melting snow as we hiked. This is the best time of year for woods-hiking, since the lack of forest undergrowth lets you see through to ravines, rocks, and crannies other times hidden behind summer's vegetation.

The upland woods we'd entered was once an oak savanna, not a woods at all. In the oak savanna, prairie grasslands were dotted by solitary, majestic oaks that could withstand prairie fire, unlike other trees. In this woods today stood a massive white oak, whose fifteen-foot circumference bespoke 350 years of growth. Its lateral branches had spread at a time when there was no other forest competition. "It's been bent, burnt, and struck by lightning," Bob said, admiring the massive tree, still healthy despite bearing a lifetime of scars.

Finally we emerged at one of the overlooks not usually seen by visitors who stick to the trails. Here Whitewater Creek slices right-angle corners as it enters the preserve from the north. Beneath us lay scattered boulders at the base of the 200-foot sheer bluff, with cave entrances tucked away on the valley floor. Bob urged me to take in the view from the lip of a chimney rock, cautioning care as I inched along the icy, snowy ledges. The only other prints in the snow belonged to a bobcat, who undoubtedly had considerably more grace and balance than me. But the expansive view of the canyon, creek, forest, and other chimney rocks was worth the slow and grappling approach.

Bob gazed beyond the overlook: "No sounds, no power lines, the wildest piece of land around."

———————————

The glaciers advanced and retreated and advanced, crunching their way down from the Arctic. Beyond the glacier's edge—at nearby Whitewater–Lost Canyon—winter was intense. Limestone bedrock snapped in the deep chill. The glacier crept forward a few miles.

Summer came. Summer was summer, a bit cooler than today, but green and lush here just beyond the ice. The glacier melted back a few miles. Perhaps mastodons foraged nearby, perhaps the earliest Paleo-Americans entered in search of prey.

Summers, by and by, grew warmer, the winters a bit less intense. Meltwater swelled the creeks and rivers—cutting, downcutting—

even beyond the glacier itself, and much of it funneled into the under ground chambers.

In 2006, hikers, hunters, and wildlife enthusiasts were abuzz over the acquisition of Whitewater Canyon. But there was more to come. In July 2007, an adjacent 144-acre property known as Lost Canyon (or Valley of Thirteen Caves) was purchased from Dick and Arlene Henneberry as a wildlife preserve to be operated by the Jones County Conservation Board. Once again, hunting and conservation groups, businesses, and individuals quickly coalesced to raise funds for the purchase.

With the two properties side by side, the respective conservation boards are working to create a seamless combined preserve.

On a just-warm-enough, sunny, late autumn afternoon, my wife Dianne and I set out to explore the newly acquired Lost Canyon. If the Whitewater trails mostly take hikers through the uplands, the trail into Lost Canyon takes us down into the valley, in search of the Thirteen Caves. A long grassland trail, sloping southwest from the parking lot, marches us first past a series of ledges and shale outcrop-pings as we descend.

Then the trail shifts northward again, and one by one the caves reveal themselves in the limestone bluff faces on either side of the valley floor. We enter a few of the larger ones, breathing in the damp, musky smell of the darkened earth.

"Geologists are impressed with the pristine condition of Lost Canyon," says Jones County Conservation Board Director Larry Gullett, crediting the Henneberry's and their ancestors who'd owned the property since 1845 with having been great stewards of the land. He sees his role, and the public's, as continuing that stewardship. For example, visitors need to take great care when entering caves in order to avoid disturbing active (still forming) formations. There is, for example, a "splash cup" formation on one of the cave floors, and an inadvertent step could put an end to millions of years of natural growth.

Henneberry had frequently explored the valley, caves, and adjacent Whitewater Creek as a youth. "We explored everywhere, including places we shouldn't have gone," like Gray's Hole in Whitewater Creek, a place of dangerous eddies. Claustrophobic by nature, Dick didn't enter crawl spaces in the caves, but later on, his son did. Through the years Dick grazed cattle in the valley—which kept the undergrowth in check—and hunted and held family trail rides, picnics, and berry-picking expeditions.

Henneberry remembers Cliff Waller as a good neighbor, and said when Waller sold Whitewater as a wildlife refuge, "That's what got me interested in doing the same for Lost Canyon. It's just like having an antique car. You want people to be able to look at it."

Today, Dianne and I are reaping the benefits of the property's preservation, flitting back and forth across the valley, checking out caves on either side. Some of the larger caves extend sixty feet into the limestone before being choked by sediment, says Gullett. It's nice to know, but I am in no way tempted to check it out for myself.

The limestone bluffs reveal the story of their Ordovician beginnings in the fossil record. Corals, cephalopods, brachiopods, and colonial algae once thrived in the warm, ancient seas that washed over the region, contributing their shells and lime to the gathering muck on the sea floor. Compacted and chemically altered into bedrock and then raised along with the general upswell of the continent, the sea fossils now occasionally surprise the hiker at 800 feet above and a thousand miles away from today's sea level.

The canyon offers other surprises as well. Tiny spring-fed brooks in the valley offer unusual flora due to the moist but well-drained environment, including mosses and maidenhair fern that grows inordinately thick. Numerous freshwater springs coupled with the sloping terrain create a lush environment. "It smells like a greenhouse there in spring," says Gullett.

Flora and shelter attract fauna. Gullett has noted eastern phoebes nesting in the caves, wild turkeys, pheasants, and scarlet tanagers. "It is a paradise for groundhogs, woodchucks, coyote, fox, and white-tailed deer," says Gullett.

Some of the surprises are man-made. A 1935 CCC plaque marks

a rock-dam soil conservation device designed to stem erosion on a steep ravine leading into the valley. Jackson County, says Gullett, included some of the first soil conservation districts in the state of Iowa, and the Henneberry family were leaders in the movement. Dick recalls that his father was one of the first to do contour farming. "Some people laughed at him for contouring rather than going up and down the hills," although contouring today is common practice.

Several posts mark the passage of the fifth meridian through Lost Canyon. Just after the Black Hawk War, surveyors marked out the fifth meridian—a national north-south line that bisects easternmost Iowa and from which all Iowa properties are still legally indexed. In just one month in November 1836, chief surveyor William A. Burt blazed through the Iowa bisection, but bogged down when he hit the bluff-ridden terrain of Lost Canyon.

Gullett is also laying out an "astronomical clock," marking the locations on the horizon where the sun rises on the solstices and equinoxes. These directions will be marked by aligning the posts on the meridian with a central cairn on the Whitewater property, "tying in the natural clock with the man-made features of the meridian survey."

Today, however, the slow descent toward sunset is more on our minds as we leave the canyon. At the northernmost edge of the canyon, the trail turns east again and begins a gentle ascent through a hillside prairie, headed toward the uplands. This is what autumn Sundays are made for, and we settle down onto a patch of warm grass to take in the view.

The prairie is steep-sloped and dotted with seasoned oaks. These slopes, says Gullett, were only farmed for a few years long ago, then left to revert to a more natural state. Prairie grasses and wildflowers are returning: wild sarsaparilla, blue cohosh, Virginia wild rye, bergamot. In the future, controlled burns will keep down forest encroachment and encourage native prairie.

The low angle of the sun on an autumn afternoon signals that the season is passing all too quickly, so after a good long while of just watching the prairie, Dianne and I resume the final leg of the trail back to the parking lot.

Some geologists speculate that the canyon formed twenty thousand years ago during an intermittent segment of the Wisconsinan Glacial Period. The snowfall abated temporarily, but the air was intensely cold. The extreme cold turned underground water to ice, fracturing the limestone cave structures along fissure lines and causing the main cave roof to collapse into what is now the canyon. The caves visible today probably fed into the collapsed main artery. Evidence for this collapsed-cave theory include the 90-degree turns of Lost Creek and Whitewater Creek. The sharp turns of the stream beds suggest they had been underground flows following the angular fissures of the limestone cave structure.

Or perhaps the roof blew off. This geological theory holds that meltwater sculpted the canyon twelve thousand years ago as the glaciers were retreating. Raging meltwater forced its way into underground streams and caves, following the fissure lines that typically run in right-angle patterns. The force and pressure of the rushing water blew the roof off the cave, tumbling boulders into the stream, most of which were quickly swept away.

It's hard to imagine such geologic violence here. It's hard to imagine the fatal, deafening snap of limestone cracking into the dead chill of the air, the booming collapse of the cave into its bottom stream bed. Or the relentless pressure of underground water that blew the lid off and carried away all but the largest boulders which still litter the valley floor.

It's hard to imagine because Whitewater–Lost Canyon is a quiet refuge today, with gurgling springs and gathering creeks, where cave interiors drip across the eons, where wild turkeys peck languidly for grain, and massive oaks quietly recall the prairie.

This is how the canyon presents itself today, in this blip of a moment, in geologic time. You have to listen more closely to hear the ancient collapse of bedrock.

Kickapoo Valley Reserve

The asphalt road in the valley is showing signs of wear. Grass has claimed the edges, and the pavement is crumbling here and there. But don't call the Vernon County, Wisconsin, road crews to come and patch Old 131. It's not that they're lazy or strapped for funds. It's just that Old 131 has taken on a new life as a hiking path through the 8,500-acre Kickapoo Valley Reserve.

Which is a reprieve from its prior destination as the lake bottom had the Kickapoo River been dammed, as once intended.

The Kickapoo River covers sixty miles as the crow flies through southwest Wisconsin, but it meanders for 106 miles within the region. The name derives from the Algonquin language, meaning literally "he who goes here, then there," but is translated more colloquially as "crooked river." The largest river entirely within the Driftless Land, it drains a watershed of a half-million acres, with 500 miles of tributaries. Undisturbed by the last great glaciers, the Kickapoo may be one of the world's oldest river systems.

Undoubtedly, Old State Highway 131 has been underwater before. The Kickapoo is prone to downstream flooding where the valley widens, due to steep-sided upstream sandstone walls, cascading hills, and its 140 watershed tributaries. Old farming and land management practices contributed to flooding in the early years as well: non-contour farming funneled runoff into the river, cattle-grazing on the steep hillsides compacted the soil so that rain and snowmelt could no longer easily soak in, and clear-cutting of timber robbed the land of thirsty roots that could soak up a good rain in summer. The Kickapoo flooded downstream towns like La Farge, Viola, Readstown, and Soldiers Grove in 1935, 1948, 1951, 1956, and 1961. By the early 1960s, state and local politicians decided that something needed to be done, and the La Farge Dam flood-control project was born.

By 1969 the federal government was purchasing the first of 149 farms to be affected by the dam and lake. Some property owners were reluctant to sell, but were forced to do so by the inevitable sweep of "progress." The Army Corps of Engineers began construction, and by 1975 the dam was half completed.

And then the plug came out.

One hundred forty-nine family names are inscribed in the limestone façade of the visitor center at the Kickapoo Valley Reserve, the first feature I noticed when I arrived on a cloudy April afternoon. These were the plain folk who had sacrificed their farms—willingly or not—for the 1,780-acre lake and hydroelectric dam that never came to be.

A short hike from the visitor center lays bare the original intent. Down past the steep, pine-filled slopes above the river, down into the soggy valley where the season's last snow has just recently melted but the ground hasn't thawed enough to soak it in, down to the swelling Kickapoo where the freshly awakened frogs are having a coming-out party, it seems at first that this will be a fairly typical hike in the hills and stream valleys of the Driftless Land.

But at the distant edge of the valley stands a 110-foot tower. You might guess, from a far-off glance, that is an old fire watchtower, but that would make no sense because its base is on the valley floor instead of some grand overlook. Or from a distance you might guess it a grain silo, but the shape is all wrong. It is instead the grey, concrete dam tower constructed in the early 1970s but never pressed into action, and now it is a bit weathered with age.

The hiking path leads to Old 131 on the valley floor. New State Highway 131 runs smartly along or near the eastern boundary of the Reserve on higher ground that would have overlooked the lake. But the old route, growing wilder with the absence of traffic, winds through the valley, crosses a newly constructed covered-bridge, and then climbs the next hillside where it escapes the Reserve boundaries and becomes what it once was, a functioning road bearing traffic to nearby La Farge.

I climb into the grasslands above the road. It is quiet and isolated here. Smart people aren't hiking when the ground and the sky appear equally saturated. I imagine this field as a high pasture, but a wall of sloping rocks just off in the distance brings me back to the present. High in this old field, the dam structure is born at ground level and gathers bulk as the hilltop grassland slopes down to the valley some 150 feet below.

But the dam doesn't close off valley. Construction halted before it shut down the Kickapoo. Viewed from the top of the dam, the valley stretches out, grassy and brown in early April, in either direction, north and south. The Kickapoo runs freely.

Clouds were gathering on the dam proponents in 1970. On the one hand, the Army Corps of Engineers had made significant progress. The dam was about 40 percent complete. Eighteen million dollars had already been spent. Another estimated $20 million would have completed the structure. The new lake would bring tourists, and the dam would help downstream townspeople sleep at night when the Kickapoo was rising in its banks.

But the 1970 Environmental Protection Act threw cold water on the dam. Thirteen rare or endangered plant species grace the grounds, including woodland cudweed, cream gentian, bird's eye primrose, and 47 percent of Wisconsin's northern monkshood. Threatened or endangered animal species include wood turtles, ornate box turtles, the Eastern Massasauga snake, and the bald eagle, along with rare birds like the red-shouldered hawk.

At about the same time, archaeologists discovered important

Native American cultural sites in the area. Sandstone petroglyphs included three bird-human figures depicting perhaps costumed humans or spirits, a human figure in a boat, and another human beside a dwelling or teepee. Rock shelters revealed four distinct dwelling periods between 1500 BC and 1000 AD. Campsite artifacts suggested Native American presence for fur hunting and fire ceremonies. Burial mounds evidenced the Hopewellian Culture Native Americans.

In 1971, the Sierra Club filed suit to stop construction of the dam, although the suit was thrown out of court. But the negatives were flooding the valley. In1974, a University of Wisconsin study indicated that the proposed lake would never fill to the depth the Corps of Engineers had projected. Delays and cost overruns now meant that $51 million (not $20 million) would be required to complete the job. Political support at the state and federal level waned, then evaporated.

Perhaps no one of the issues on its own would have burst the dam, says Kickapoo Valley Reserve Executive Director Marcy West, but the combination of concerns created "a perfect storm" that led the Army Corps of Engineers to put the project on hold in 1975, pending further study.

For twenty years the land sits idle.

In Orwellian 1984, nine years after work is suspended on the dam, the Corps demolishes the bridges on Old 131 to halt its use as a road for local traffic. A feasibility study for a smaller dam also turns up negative. The costs exceed the benefits.

The community is furious that the project is heading nowhere. With the forced purchase of 149 farms, over a hundred families have been displaced, many of whom have moved out of the county. The local school district loses about a hundred students, and businesses suffer in La Farge and other area towns. Anticipated new dollars from recreational spending by visitors to the proposed lake are no longer on the horizon.

Real storm clouds.

Marcy West understands the community's hard feelings, but also the need for healing and moving on. And she knows first-hand the good being accomplished at the Reserve.

Healing is a gradual process, but an important early step took place in 1992 when Wisconsin Governor Tommy Thompson convened a Citizen Advisory Committee to focus on what could be done with the land rather than dwell on what had been done. Many local residents would have preferred to return the properties to the original owners or their children. But since the land had been purchased by the federal government, legal procedures would have required the properties to be sold at auction. And returning the land to its agricultural past would not have addressed the flooding problems.

Other proposals surfaced, including developing the grounds as a national park, but locals had had enough of the federal government's intervention by then.

In 1993, the Citizen Advisory Committee finally proposed that the land be turned into a state-owned nature reserve with low-impact tourism and educational programs, and that a portion of the land be deeded back to the Ho-Chunk nation, which had populated the area prior to the arrival of European-Americans. The concept got the go-ahead from local communities and the state of Wisconsin.

Faced with mounting pressure to do something, the federal government finally de-authorized the Corps' dam project in 1996 as part of the Water Resources Development Act.

In so doing, Congress designated that 8,569 acres be deeded to the State of Wisconsin and 1,200 acres deeded to the Ho-Chunk nation. A Memorandum of Understanding between them stipulated that the entire grounds be administered as a single reserve with access to the public.

On the Trust Lands, the Ho-Chunk have re-established native grassland, undertaken timber and grasslands management, introduced language immersion programs, offered tours, and more.

In 1996, the Kickapoo Reserve Management Board hired Marcy West as its Executive Director. The Kickapoo Valley Reserve is funded through the Wisconsin state forestry program, grants, trail fees, sustainable timber harvest, and farm rentals in certain parcels.

The Friends of the Kickapoo Valley Reserve also raise funds, donate labor, and offer educational programs. In 2004, the Management Board rebuilt three bridges on Old 131 as hiking bridges across the Kickapoo, and the Friends added a roof to "#18," giving it the appearance of an old-fashioned covered bridge.

By 2004, the Army Corps of Engineers had funded construction of new State Highway 131 on the ridge above the valley, some ten years after removing bridges on the old road.

In the same year, the 8,300 square foot visitor center was completed at the Reserve, its construction including thirty-one trees cut down in the road project. The center has been visited by ten thousand tourists each year since then, and is frequented by the local population and area students as well.

To help compensate for the loss of private property taxes, the state of Wisconsin makes payments (Aid in Lieu of Taxes) to the area schools, towns, county, and technical college.

Nature heals in curious ways, too, when left to itself, and in the twenty years the land sat idle, the Kickapoo's flooding problems have lessened, though have not disappeared. Trees rebounded on the steep slopes, their thirsty roots ready to soak up rain and snowmelt. Grassland replaced plowed fields to the same effect. And the absence of developed land in the Reserve means that the flooding within its boundaries does not create an economic disaster. It is a classic case of a "no-build alternative," says West. "Folks in La Farge do believe that having the 8,500 acres above them helped absorb some of the flood's impact" in 2007, when high waters once again raced down the Kickapoo.

Even so, at times local residents must still wonder "what could have been" if the dam had been built. The 2008 summer floods that devastated much of the Midwest likewise washed through the Kickapoo Valley.

West acknowledges the mixed feelings toward the reserve in the community. The ATV community is upset that they can't ride the hills like they had when it was privately owned or during the years it was in limbo with the federal government. Some former landowners are still bitter about having been forced to sell.

But West hopes that the "next generation"—the grandchildren and great-grandchildren of the former landowners—will have a different perspective, and she sometimes sees them hiking, bicycling, and fishing on the Reserve. And even some of the landowners themselves have "realized it as a hardship they faced and then have moved on with their lives," says West.

I asked Marcy what I thought was a throw-away question, as I was confused on a matter of terminology. "What is the difference between a 'reserve' and a 'refuge'?" I wondered, having heard the different terms used for different places. The difference, West was quick to point out, is quite pronounced. "A reserve is meant to be a protected area," she explained, "but one that allows for low-impact tourism."

The Kickapoo Valley Reserve offers:

- Twenty-five miles of paved roads or twenty-four miles of off-road trails for bicycling;
- Thirty-seven miles of horseback-riding trails;
- Twenty-five camping sites;
- Canoeing and kayaking amid the sandstone bluffs and rock outcroppings;
- Hunting, fishing, and trapping within established seasons;
- Cross-country skiing, snowshoeing, and snowmobiling;
- The Dam Challenge Triathlon, held each October, with seven miles canoeing, fourteen miles road-biking, and a three-mile cross-country run;
- Hiking trails that lead to impressive overlooks and past archaeological features such as Native American rock shelters.

The Reserve meets its educational mission through a number of programs involving school group visits, adult education, Saturday-and-evening programs, and week-long summer programs for students, teachers, and other adults. In the summer, depending on your age and interests, you might set out for "Exploring the Outdoor

Classroom," "GPS in the Kickapoo Valley Reserve," or "Adventure Day Camps," among other activities.

———————————

Oak, maple, hickory, old growth pine, hemlock. Woodland cudweed, cream gentian, rock club moss, bird's eye primrose, northern monkshood, angelica, New England aster, wild bergamot, broad-leaved cattail, horseweed, jack-in-the pulpit, Jacobs ladder, May apple, wild columbine, yellow coneflower. White-tail deer, fox squirrel, coyote, beaver, river otter, snapping turtle, garter snake, bull snake, bull frog, spring-peeper frog, American Toad. Canada goose, wood duck, mallard, ring-necked pheasant, wild turkey, ruffed grouse, great blue heron, turkey vulture, bald eagle, cooper's hawk, red-shouldered hawk, golden eagle, American kestrel, killdeer, barred owl, long-eared owl, ruby-throated hummingbird, belted kingfisher, pileated woodpecker, marsh wren, scarlet tanager.

These are but a few of the thousands of plant and animal species identified at Kickapoo Valley Reserve.

———————————

The few spits of rain turn to heavy sprinkles as I descend the hillside where the partially completed dam originates. The covered bridge offers refuge for a few minutes, the rain drops drumming on the tin roof, but when it's clear that it's not going to let up, I resume my way on Old 131. Where the road passes between two wetland ponds, a pair of white egrets gracefully wade and peck at their watery lunch on the left, and a honking goose creates a ruckus to the right. Cattails line the marshy shorelines, and a red-winged blackbird—my first sighting of the spring—watches me suspiciously from an old fence post. Hills and bluffs a half a mile away barely poke through the foggy mist.

The rain picks up. I find my footing carefully on a water-soaked path leading back to the visitor center, but even at the trail's edge where the surface is grassy and apparently dry, the soil gurgles under my boot steps. I'm drenched when I reach the car and take off for home.

The Kickapoo River is wild and blustery. And well within its banks.

The Army Corps of Engineers once envisioned fishing boats and water skiers on the surface of a 1,780-acre lake in the Kickapoo Valley. Beneath it—submerged—would lie sandstone bluffs, hilly terrain, Native American archaeological sites, habitat for rare and endangered plants and animals, the original river bed of the meandering Kickapoo, and, of course, Old 131.

Instead, the valley today teems with life. There are human voices in the valley and an ornery, honking goose. And that is enough.

Summer Here

*A sweet summer afternoon. Cool breezes
and a clear sky. This day will not come
again.*

—Thomas Merton,
Conjectures of a Guilty Bystander

Today my bicycle odometer hit 500 miles for the year on the afternoon before Memorial Day. The first 500 were the season's warm-up,
since I typically ride about 3,000 miles a year. By tomorrow—Memorial Day—summer will be underway, at least in my own definition.

Summer in the Driftless Land celebrates heat and sweat. When
the sun-baked river bluff shimmers heat waves, it is hard to know
which is real—the sharp, scratching entrenchments of rock or the
illusory flicker. Summer sweat and peeled clothing blur the edges
between the body and the air, between breath and spirit. The earth
breathes a humid sigh, the skin bathes in a salty sea.

But every summer offers occasional reprieves when you can leave
the bedroom windows open at night and feel the cool breezes brush
over you. Morning mists will coil in the Mississippi valley, shrouding
a barge hounding upriver and unleashing a pair of geese who burst
from the fog, intent on the backwater woods.

There will be storms. Tornadoes will punctuate the season here
and there: this year has been particularly deadly and devastating.
Increasingly, early-summer floods wash down the Mississippi and its
tributaries. But an isolated shower is a blessed gift and best received

on the front porch swing, served up with memories of your once-young children nestled in the crook of your arm.

With my children grown, however, bicycling now defines summer in the Driftless for me. On Saturday mornings, my bicycle group gathers at my front porch at 7 a.m. for coffee and a recap of the week before the ride begins. Our routes vary, but one of our favorites is a forty-mile spin to Breitbach's Restaurant in Balltown just north of Dubuque. The ride will take us from the bluff ridge where I live, down to the flats along the river, and back up into the highlands north of Dubuque. At the top of a mile-long climb—the first of several on the route—Jim will do a perfect imitation of Thurston Howell from Gilligan's Island (betraying our baby-boomer status), saying "Lovie, I do believe there's water on my brow." At Breitbach's—Iowa's oldest restaurant—the common order will be an omelet "bigger than your head," but mine will be the raspberry pie, piled an inch-and-a half thick, sweet and fruity. These rides—the miles, the hills, and especially the pies—will prepare us for RAGBRAI, the "[Des Moines] Register's Annual Great Bicycle Ride Across Iowa."

But I will ride on my own as well, half an hour to an hour a day throughout the summer, my own monastery of silent, solitary thought amid the hills of the Mines of Spain or along the eastern shore of the Mississippi in southwest Wisconsin. My thoughts will bounce around from school to family to observations about the wind speed and direction. I can go mindless, without thought, Zen-like, and return to consciousness a mile later, wondering how it was that nothing—not even sight impressions—registered during the past five minutes. On the most challenging hills, I will count pedal strokes. One hundred strokes on the mark will take me from the Catfish Creek bridge to the top of the hill, though my heart rate and breathing will take another minute to catch up. Sweet, salty sweat bathes my back and hair.

I usually ride hard, for exercise and obsessing over the "average speed" function on my odometer, but for a more leisurely summer's affair, my wife and I will go canoeing. In the Mississippi, we put in at Massey Station just south of town and paddle across a side-channel to Nine Mile Island Slough, where we ease up and listen to the bird chatter in the backwater woods. Before the afternoon is through, a couple of bass will break the water and a carp will roll its lumbering back just beneath the river's surface. The pea-green water barely moves through the slough in the languid heat, and the river bottom is a pasty, black mud, no doubt washed down from some of the finest farm fields upstream. If we want a bit of sand, we'll head slightly north to the tip of Nine Mile Island and find some smooth-worn driftwood.

Hiking fills another summer niche, although in many ways, fall and winter hikes are better, when the days are chilly, the mosquitoes are gone, and the lack of undergrowth lets you see deeper into the woods, revealing rock outcroppings and the rare Native American burial mound or a long abandoned lead-mine pit. Even so, the droning flies and the thick-growing forest floor on a summer's hike are constant reminders of the sweaty lushness of life.

We tent-camped more when we were first married and childless, and when the kids were little, than we do now. A couple of nights at Governor Dodge State Park—in the middle of the Driftless in Wisconsin—included bike rides through the 5,000-acre park, hiking to Stephens Falls, canoeing and swimming in the man-made Cox Hollow Lake. We lay our sleeping bags directly on the tent floor. The family joke goes that my favorite mattress would be a cement pad. There is something good about a morning's waking where you raise yourself up from an earthen bed rather than lower your feet down onto a bedroom floor. No one looks forward to the Empty Nest Syndrome when the kids have all left home, but I suspect that a return to simple camping will be one of the tradeoffs.

You don't need to leave the yard to experience a Driftless summer, though. A backyard fire-pot for summer campfires will do just fine. As night descends, a couple of wax-and-sawdust sticks ignite the sticks and twigs gathered after the recent storm, making a bed of glowing, red-hot coals to inflame the logs cut from last year's tree thinning or hauled in from a friend's farm. On the best evenings, a few neighbors drop by and Dianne or the kids come out back for a while, but it's still a good night when my only fireside companion is the book I'm reading. A cold beer tops it off.

In the frontyard, the Driftless summer is defined by the fruit from the dwarf cherry tree. In spring I'll snap a couple of photos of the cherry-blossom flowers and slightly regret their dropping, but regrets are short-lived when early summer offers promise of a full bounty in the form of the tight green cherry buds. When they ripen—usually around the Fourth of July but later this year due to the late spring—I'll haul the stepladder out and find to my simultaneous delight and dismay that the top of the dwarf tree has just now grown slightly beyond my farthest stretch, and a handful of cherries will have to be abandoned to the neighborhood birds.

Now the cherries are a dark red, their skins firm and warm in the sun. But you can still feel the juicy meat beneath the skin, the total effect a bit like a miniature water balloon. Swipe a few for eating while you pick, if you like sour cherries, although the sun-warmed fruit still on the tree will be sweeter later when they're chilled. Sweet, sticky juice—the elixir of summer—runs down my arms while I pick, and later when I pit the cherries in the kitchen, I'll inevitably squirt the juices about the table, chairs, and floor nearby. No one else in the family likes the sour fruit, so I can be as selfish as I want, after sharing the bounty with neighbors. These cherries will become fresh toppings for breakfast cereal or ice cream or become the meat for a homemade cherry pie. The excess are stashed into zip-lock bags and frozen, to be thawed in winter, the bounty of the summer sun's delayed release.

This is summer in the Driftless Land. As a teacher, I have more time off in summer than most people, although less than most people suppose I have, as my job also includes many non-teaching summer duties. My summer time off is dearly paid for in weekend and night-time work during the school year. But these are precious months no matter what your occupation. When late June brings the summer solstice, the warmth of summer will still build for a couple of months, but the almost imperceptible shortening of daylight hours throws us a psychological punch as we realize that the days are indeed beginning their long slide again toward winter.

But not just yet. I've still a couple of thousand miles to bicycle up and down these Driftless hills before it's time to call it a season. I'll eat a lot and drink a few beers, and sweat them out on these rides, lose a few pounds, and bask in the summer sun.

The Savanna Army Depot:
What Lies Buried

Morning mists roil just before sunup on this mid-May dawn, concealing the Mississippi River valley hidden beneath. But by the time the sun gains the horizon at 5:45 a.m., as I turn off Highway 84 onto the former grounds of the Savanna (Illinois) Army Depot, the mist has largely dissipated and the valley lies exposed.

I am going mist-netting and bird-banding with Dan Wenny of the Illinois Natural History Survey (INHS) at the Lost Mound Field Station, located within the old depot grounds along the Mississippi River in northwest Illinois. The task at hand is to track bird species; today we are studying whether the grasshopper sparrow is increasing or decreasing on the sand prairie, in the former home of bombs.

It is an intriguing, exciting, and troubling place, depending on the story one unearths out here on the prairie. I could tell you about the Army Depot, once employing over seven thousand civilians at its peak during World War II, and then shrinking, edict by edict, until its closure in March 2000. Or I could tell you about the 9,000-plus acres of wildlife refuge harboring forty-seven threatened or endangered species of plants and animals and the largest sand-prairie remnant in the state of Illinois. There is a story to be told about three thousand acres of hoped-for economic rebirth. Or should I tell another story, this one about buried contaminants, an environmental clean-up site that could cost taxpayers up to $300 million?

Over here there are coneflowers. Over there you had better not step. Just where does the treasure lie, and where does one find poison?

This morning is pure treasure. Along with Josh, his student intern, Wenny is setting mist nets, wispy black badminton-like nets strung between upright poles in the hopes that grasshopper sparrows will absent-mindedly fly into and temporarily entangle themselves until the INHS specialist retrieves them, charts their measurements, and places an identification band on their legs before releasing them. For the prairie is returning, re-establishing itself on a unique ground, and Wenny wants to know what, in turn, is happening to the wildlife here.

But there are other intrigues to chart as well. What happens to a community when its largest historical employer—the Army—packs up and leaves town? What happens when the government leaves behind an environmental mess and a clean-up process that is painstakingly slow? What happens when creative thinkers are unleashed to create a wildlife refuge and rebuild the economic base? And what if this story is played out time and time again at hundreds of closed military installations across the country?

———————————

The Savanna Army Depot story begins after the onset of World War I. The U.S. Congress, recognizing the need for permanent war-readiness, authorized, among other facilities, a Midwest "proving grounds" for test-firing weapons and artillery. In 1917, according to a study conducted by nearby Augustana College historians, the 13,000-acre Savanna site was chosen for several reasons. The area was not adjacent to any cities, yet was only sixty miles from the Rock Island (Illinois) Arsenal that produced many of the large guns to be tested. The sandy riverside prairie was less agriculturally productive than the prevailing rich, black Midwestern soil, and therefore less sought-after by farmers. The river bottomland with its sloughs and myriad islands provided a buffer from river traffic, but the railroad passing at its eastern boundary would offer good means of importing machinery and resources and exporting munitions.

The base officially opened in December 1918, and the artillery began to fly. Many of the munitions fired were blanks, with a focus on testing the accuracy and distance of the weaponry, not the munitions themselves. But some of it was live ammo, and not all of it exploded on impact. Within a year, the base's mission was changed to storing munitions, but the months of test-firing had produced the depot's first contaminant—potentially unexploded ordnance, or UXO—that still plague the base grounds today. Before any land can be cleared for private ownership or for public access, the land has to be swept and sometimes upturned and sifted for UXO.

During the 1920s, 30s, and 40s, the depot grew, with over two hundred warehouses built to store munitions. More volatile munitions required over four hundred "igloos," i.e., steel-reinforced cement bunkers shaped somewhat like ice igloos, each with a single vertical face to house a massive steel door. The igloos ranged in size from about 1,100 to 1,800 square feet of floor space. Bulldozers plowed two feet of topsoil up over the sloping sides and roof, and grasses were planted over the tops to obscure their visibility from the air. One igloo blew up in 1948, leaving a crater one hundred feet wide and fifty feet deep, still apparent today. The blast registered on seismograph recordings 120 miles away in Chicago, and Savanna and Hanover locals reported blown-out windows and cracked plaster. The four-ton steel door was never found. Local lore puts it somewhere at the bottom of the Mississippi.

And so it went out on the prairie, where anyone who didn't want to work on the farm could usually find work at the depot, and many did both. Still, depot activity increased and declined according to the military needs of each generation. In 1939, only 143 civilians worked at the depot, but that figure rocketed to 7,195 by 1942, 36 percent of whom were female, the renowned Rosie the Riveters of World War II. Civilian employees lived in hastily constructed rows of apartments in the quiet nearby towns of Hanover and Savanna, or commuted from towns an hour or more drive away.

During World War II, the depot's mission expanded to include production and recycling of munitions, and later included a training school for maintenance and handling of munitions. Depot employees prided themselves on their work; munitions shipped from the depot were stamped S.O.D. (Savanna Ordnance Depot), and soldiers frequently sent word of appreciation for the job well-done. The bombs used in the Jimmy Doolittle Raid, the first U.S. retaliation on Japan after Pearl Harbor, were produced at and shipped from the Savanna Depot.

After World War II, the depot entered a slow decline, although each new military engagement produced a bubble of employment. The 1950s typically engaged about 2,000 civilian workers; by the 1960s the number stood at 1,000; in 1974 there were 750, and in 1995, when the depot was placed on the Base Realignment and Closure (BRAC) list, the number of workers had dwindled to 450.

Clouds were gathering out on the prairie. In 1977, the depot was first considered for closure, but local businessmen banded together and successfully lobbied Washington to keep it open. The inevitable finally occurred, however, when a new BRAC was formed under rules preventing individual bases on the list being "rescued" by Congress. The Savanna Army Depot was placed on the list in 1995, and closure occurred in 2000.

The closing of the Savanna Depot is a story echoed across the country. At least ninety-seven major installations have been closed nationwide since 1988, and another thirty-three were included in a closure plan submitted in 2005, each presenting some mixture of environmental and economic problems and opportunities. It would be easy for an isolated outpost like Savanna to get lost in the shuffle.

A drive-through of the Savanna Depot grounds today reveals a ghost town of abandoned military buildings here on the prairie, surrounded by farms, river bluffs, and the steadfast Mississippi River. Today I enter the grounds past the offices of the Local Redevelopment Authority (LRA), cross the railroad tracks into the compound and find—mostly abandoned—the security office, fire station, NCO barracks, gym and recreation center, mess hall, bowling alley, commissary, theater, pool, and Officers Club (spelled "Officer's Club"). Environmental clean-up activities were, until recently, directed from the Headquarters building, and new businesses now occupy the ammunitions school, commander's and second-in-command's houses, and a fraction of the two-hundred-plus warehouses and storage buildings. In an effort to make the grounds more welcoming, the guard house has recently been removed, as well as an old army sign that once warned: "All persons, their possessions, and vehicles are liable to search upon entering, during their stay, or upon leaving this installation."

The immediate impact of the depot closure on the nearby towns of Hanover and Savanna was muted somewhat because employee numbers had been dwindling for decades, and because many of the remaining workers were at or near retirement age. Still, the local populations suffered. From the 1980 to the 2000 census (by which time many workers had already left), Hanover lost nearly 200 of its previous 1,000 residents; Savanna, slightly larger, lost 1,000 of its 4,500.

But towns survive and people find work. I met Marty Sheehy and Marty Altensey, two long-time depot workers who found employment at one of the first new businesses on the grounds, one morning in March 2004. Proud of their work, past and present, they had stories to tell, building on and sometimes correcting each other's memories. Sheehy, a thirty-five-year employee of the depot, had dutifully crossed the river every day from Bellevue, Iowa, to work in the machine shop, where he eventually became chief of the Ammunition Peculiar Equipment (A.P.E.) shop. A skilled machinist, Sheehy built A.P.E. to test the shelf-life of ammunition by exploding samples inside a safebox, x-ray machines to test ammunition for defects, and hundreds more specially-designed A.P.E. for a variety of purposes. Sheehy had now found work in the same machine shop for Stickle Warehousing, doing repairs and special orders for the business' truck and ocean fleet and for other local businesses.

Marty Altensey, a twenty-three-year employee of the depot, had worked mostly in inventory and stock, unloading ammunition into igloos and warehouses, and loading it again onto trains and trucks for shipping. He unloaded mustard gas from the igloos when it was shipped to Colorado for disposal. He worked on the ammunition lines, retrieving usable TNT from old, obsolete projectiles for use in new weaponry. He drove a fork lift, loading weapons for Desert Shield and Desert Storm. He helped detonate and destroy old, decaying weapons. He, too, had now found work with Stickle Warehousing, one of the first fruits of economic development.

For Sheehy and Altensey, depot memories were never far removed from their new jobs. "There are still pictures back in the machine shop from the army days," says Sheehy, "photos of people from back then, an old phone book. You come in to work, see the fire station, the two smoke stacks from the factory areas, and it gets to you."

Altensey agrees. "You get back in a storage area, you see someone's name written on a wall and think, 'I remember him.' I expect to see a guard at the entryway. Now it's like a ghost town."

———————————

We load the INHS pickup with supplies for the morning's mist netting. Poles and nets, charts for data entry, and Wenny's fishing-tackle box with its supply of leg bands, banding pliers for handling the tiny bands, measuring instruments, solutions for securing the leg bands, etc. "The guys at the hardware store know not to ask me anymore what I'm using the stuff for," he jokes. "They had a field day when I said I was catching sparrows."

Out in the pickup, the windshield fogs against the morning's still-brisk air. We detour en route to the study area, around a "demolition circle" from the 1930s which is being cleaned of the contaminants left behind when obsolete weapons were disassembled, detonated, and sometimes burned. On the detour we pass hundreds of empty igloos. Today a deer races down from the top of one of the igloos as we pass.

At the prairie site, Dan and Josh set up about ten mist nets, usually around aromatic sumac bushes, where grasshopper sparrows often perch and sing. Most of the nets are set out singly in a variety of locations within a short walk, but two or three are set at angles to each other around larger bushes. The birds fly into the netting from their various perches and get entangled. "They're easier to catch in early spring when the males chase each other around and don't notice the net," Wenny says. Later in the season, Wenny uses "Frank," a stuffed grasshopper sparrow accompanied by a CD of a male bird song, to lure his catches. Other sparrows will come to chase it away, attack it, and get caught in the netting. "Frank's had to be sewn up a number of times," Wenny grins.

Dan easily identifies bird calls. "That buzzy trill is the grasshopper sparrow's song," he says. The prairie is seeing an increasing population among many of its bird species since the closing of the depot. The grasshopper sparrow, however, is in comparative decline, but ironically its decline signifies the prairie's recovery. The sparrow, a short-grass bird, was well-adapted to the well-clipped turf of the army days when cattle were grazed in and around the igloos to reduce the chances of prairie fire. Cattle grazing was discontinued in 1999. Since then, tall-grass species have grown back to full stature, and tall-grass birds have increased in population.

The first bird entangled in the net is a male grasshopper sparrow, already banded in 2002. Dan marks the location of the catch on his map and then measures the bird. Wing length: 63 mm. The tail measures 45 mm, the leg 19.7 mm. He measures its fat deposit near the sternum: not much in spring, but by fall the bird will have stored up fat for migration. Its bill measures 12.7 mm in length, 5.4 mm in width, 6.1 mm in depth. Wenny puts the bird in a cloth bag and measures its weight at 18 grams. He checks for parasites and finds small mites on the wings, not unusual. He inspects the feathers (which wear down from abrasion and are replaced each year), but these look good. He shows Josh how to check for gender by blowing on the belly feathers. Females have a fleshy brood patch beneath the feathers that fills with blood when they are sitting on eggs, providing warmth for incubation. Finally, all measurements and checks taken, Wenny releases the bird, which flies off eagerly to a nearby sumac.

When the Savanna Depot was put on the BRAC list in 1995, the Army directed Jo Daviess and Carroll Counties to establish a non-profit Local Redevelopment Authority (LRA) to devise an economic plan for reuse of the land. This was the closure procedure typical for bases boarded up during the 1980s and 90s

Environmental and economic interests often found themselves at odds in the early post-military years. Federal agencies have first rights to request lands vacated by other federal agencies, and the United States Fish and Wildlife Service (USFWS) initially asked for 11,000 of the 13,000 acres, according to Ed Britton, current Manager of the Upper Mississippi River National Fish and Wildlife Refuge—Savanna District. "This set off an anti-fed atmosphere in the community," says Britton, as people worried that economic interests were going to be squeezed out. Unfortunately, says Britton, the USFWS was then between regional managers, and no one was there to explain that this was merely the first phase of a long negotiation.

Economic interests were hardly on the ropes, however, and the LRA hired a lawyer in its quest to obtain all the uplands as well as the lower post, where roads and existing buildings were concentrated. The first LRA board drafted an ambitious plan that included a mix of commercial development, golf courses, and upscale homes situated on top of the sand dunes adjacent to the river. Only 600 remaining acres were designated for industrial development. The Army questioned whether the reuse plan was realistic. However, they recommended the LRA let the planning phase mature and then resubmit their reuse plan within a year, says David Ylinen, a former LRA Executive Director who served after the opening phases. Later, after investigating the feasibility for major housing and green space development, the LRA determined that the original plan was probably too ambitious.

In addition, says BRAC Environmental Coordinator John Clarke, standards for environmental cleanup vary according to the use planned for the land. A residential area needs to be "clean enough for kids to play in the dirt for twenty years and not be harmed." Cleanup standards for commercial and industrial use are less rigorous, and for recreational use even less so. Thus the irony emerges that the excessive environmental contamination has made more lands available for the wildlife refuge, even though public access is severely restricted.

A second early controversy between environmentalists and economic interests stemmed from members of the first LRA who wanted to build a prison on the depot grounds. According to Bob Wehrle, who describes himself as one of the few early LRA members who "took the environmental perspective to blend economic development and preservation," the issue wasn't *whether* a prison was appropriate use of the land, but *where* it ought to be located. A region on the southern end of the depot, or south post, had been identified for economic development because it already had some basic infrastructure, with roads, water and electrical service, and many existing buildings.

However, says Wehrle, environmentalists were stunned when then-Illinois-Governor James Edgar announced that the northern sand prairie would house what would soon be dubbed, derisively, as the "prison on the prairie." The site selection was particularly distasteful to environmentalists, as it would not only destroy the rare sand prairie but would also disrupt the largest uninterrupted continuum of bio-regions—from river bottomland to prairie to wooded blufflands—along the entire upper Mississippi River valley. The site also contained James' clammyweed, an endangered plant species.

Environmentalists suspected the motives of the prison proponents. Placing the prison in the upper sand prairie would remove it from the southern economic zone, whose development might be hampered by the inclusion of a prison.

But most of all, the three self-identified LRA environmentalists—Wehrle, John Rutherford, and Jim Rachuy—were dismayed over the process. The prairie site had never been discussed and agreed upon by the full LRA board. Soon another local resident, Harry Drucker, helped form the Friends of the Depot—which Wehrle, Rutherford, and Rachuy joined—and secured legal help from the Environmental Law and Policy Center in Chicago. The environmental lawyers discovered that the original LRA Director (prior to Ylinen) and a few additional members had obtained and submitted application forms to the Illinois Department of Corrections (IDOC) requesting the prison be considered for this site. Drucker says the Friends were "outraged that the decision-making had been done secretly, behind closed doors."

The Friends began writing letters to government officials and alerted the *Chicago Tribune* to the matter. The new revelations and environmental concerns caused the governor to drop his endorsement of the prison proposal. The governor shifted the location of the prison site to the nearby town of Thomson, Illinois, away from the depot but still within commuting distance for potential workers from the community.

For several years the newly constructed 1600-bed prison stood empty, save for a single security watchguard, due to state budget cuts in prison funding. By 2008—seven years after its completion—the facility housed only 140 inmates and provided employment for seventy-two individuals, rather than the six hundred anticipated jobs. But by 2009-2010, the prison had worked its way back into the center of controversy as the proposed site for relocation of Guantanamo Bay detainees.

When the Prison-on-the-Prairie controversy was at its height, the original LRA had met an impasse between those members with environmental interests and those more singly focused on economic development. For harmony's sake, the Jo Daviess and Carroll County boards reconfigured the LRA membership, a move that had been planned anyway to transition from a "planning LRA" to an "implementation LRA," and the new board began making headway. A few more plan drafts were made and a few land trades occurred. They finally agreed on the current distribution of land. Subject to environmental cleanup, the USFWS would receive 9,715 acres for the Lost Mound Unit Refuge; the Illinois Department of Natural Resources, 270 acres; the Army Corp of Engineers, 145; and the LRA, 2,947 acres for the economic zone first named Eagles Landing Development and then renamed Savanna Depot Park for Business, Industry and Technology. "Things are working cooperatively now," says Britton, and those involved in economic development tend to agree.

Several economic ventures were already underway at the depot when I first visited with business owners and planners in 2004. By 2008, a new LRA Director, Diane Komiskey, reported new names and new ventures, but was quick to point out that the average closed military facility takes about twenty-five years to be re-established for other uses. "And we're not average," she says, with the depot's status as a superfund cleanup site and the economic disadvantage of low population in Jo Daviess and Carroll counties.

Bit by bit, however, turn-around is on the horizon. One of the first developments was Stickle Warehousing, owned and operated by Rick Stickle when I visited in 2004. Stickle made the first actual land-purchase transaction at the depot. In December 2003, he presented Ylinen's LRA with a check for $948,535 for 14 warehouses on 44 acres of environmentally-clean property. Stickle also had a lease-purchase agreement for an additional 200 buildings—mostly warehouses—on the depot grounds, about 100 of which he was using to store more than 6,000 truckloads of materials.

The operations required significant re-investment. Some of the warehouses lacked electricity, so Stickle installed lines and transformers to 50 buildings at a cost of $185,000, and then wired the buildings internally, repaired masonry, sanitized and patched floors, installed safety features, and replaced overhead doors. In all, he had invested about $1.5 million in repairs and upgrades.

But these first economic fruits didn't last long. By 2009, the Stickle warehouses were no longer in operation.

Another early entrepreneur was Warren Jackman, a maritime lawyer by trade who started his international practice in 1951 and who has lived in the nearby Galena Territory for over twenty years. Jackman's office at the depot in 2004—located on the first floor of a handsome brick home formerly used by an army officer—was adorned with paintings and drawings of ships, sailors, and mermaids. But if his walls reflected his past, his thinking was poised for the future. The Burlington Northern and Santa Fe Railroad passes along the depot's eastern boundary, and 68 miles of rail track wind through the property itself, a remnant of the days when munitions would be shipped in and out of the yard by rail. Jackman seized the opportunity to create Riverport Railroad, storing excess railcars for customers of the Burlington Northern and Santa Fe.

By 2008, Riverport Railroad had 57 miles of track available that could store 2,000 railcars. In 2007, for example, the company's tracks were filled to capacity with new tanker cars that had been built for ethanol transportation but had not yet been pressed into service. Also capitalizing on the depot's rail system is RESCAR, a national company offering repair and cleaning services for railroad cars. RESCAR has become the Depot Park's largest employer, with 32 of the 53 persons currently employed on the grounds—still a far cry from the civilian employment in the glory days.

One of the most out-of-the-box developments, however, involves the igloo-shaped ammunition bunkers out on the prairie. In the aftermath of 9/11, major financial institutions and corporations recognized the need to keep back-up computer data storage far away from metropolitan sites. "Bunkertown" arose with plans to transform the old munitions bunkers into safe, secure, and survivable computer-data centers, connecting them to the outside world through fiber-optic cable and other redundant high-tech modes. The igloos' two-foot thick concrete and earthen roof cover combine to produce a cave-like, near-constant year-round cool temperature, perfect for computer facilities. And because the venture will have relatively low environmental impact, the USFWS agreed to allow the bunker project on the refuge grounds, epitomizing the current level of cooperation between environmental and economic interests. Besides, no one was quite sure what to do with the igloos. They would have been expensive to tear down, and to do so would have disturbed the prairie as much as letting them stand.

Another hi-tech entrepreneur, Gary Frederick, was drawing considerable interest by 2008. Frederick, a mechanical engineer who'd spent his career doing research and development in Arizona, retired to his family's home farm in the local hills, but "couldn't keep still," and continued with his engineering research in his home basement. By October of 2007 he'd purchased an old educational building at the Depot and had begun Fluidic Micro-controls, which designs and machines tiny air-powered sensors, controls, and actuators that can be used in micro-machining tools, aerospace business, industrial automation, etc. Another product in the works is a pneumatic pillow that can be set under micro-machines for super-stable vibration resistance.

But Frederick found himself forming another business venture when a neighboring farmer stopped in his driveway one day and proclaimed, "I want to make lightning in the back of my pickup." When the farmer explained what he meant, Frederick joked, "You've just ruined my retirement," and set out to work with the man and another farmer, another retired engineer, and a host of researchers from Northern Illinois University to develop a process by which farmers could create their own nitrogen fertilizer on-site at their farms. Using centuries-old knowledge that lightning strikes can fertilize the soil, the process involves jolting an electrical current at air passing through a tube, which separates out nitrogen from the air supply. The nitrogen is channeled into a water bath, creating nitric acid, which then can be mixed with lime to create a slurry to be spread as nitrogen fertilizer on farm fields. The slurry could replace anhydrous ammonia that must be made at commercial sites and dangerously transported to the fields. The on-site nitrogen producer, running continuously for a year, could produce enough fertilizer for a one thousand acre farm and could be powered by plugging it into the traditional electrical grid, by on-site wind energy from wind turbines small enough to be hidden in barn cupolas, or through a power-generating system that converts biomass to electricity.

If you're on my wavelength, this was all sounding too much like something out of the Jetsons. But Frederick's company, N-Ovation, has received a three-year $1 million USDA grant to work with Northern Illinois University on the biomass conversion alternative.

Frederick's vision is to create an agricultural alternative-energy center at the Depot. A half-dozen technicians from NIU were scheduled to visit the Depot to consider establishing research space at the site. Frederick noted that the fledgling N-Ovation company reflects President (then Illinois Senator) Barak Obama's victory speech after the Iowa caucuses, in which he proclaimed that the U.S. must "harness the ingenuity of farmers, scientists, and entrepreneurs to free this nation from the tyranny of oil once and for all." The N-Ovation project hits all of these fronts.

Frederick is convinced that the way to attract jobs to the Depot is to "attract professionals to the beauty of this area," as reflected in his first full-time hire, Drew Wittey, a mechanical engineering graduate from Northwestern University. Typical of a new generation of professionals, Drew likes the laidback, innovative style of a small company doing cutting-edge technology in a rural setting. Drew is the first full-time resident at the Depot Park since the closing of the military facility, as he lives in housing that formerly served married army personnel, rides his bike to the office, and works in jeans and sandals.

Other tenants had set up shop at the Depot Park by April 2008 as well, including: Bryer Productions, a photographer; Ancient Tree Builders, a cabinetry industry; BNC Bulletproof, building bullet-proof enclosures for ATMs and bank tellers; and A & B Holdings, which is converting the Commander's and Second-In-Command's houses into corporate retreat centers. Also, the non-profit Rock Island Technological Society has opened up a railroad museum and Welcome Center for the Savanna Depot Park and an Army Depot Museum as well.

The first property sale had occurred in 2003. By 2008, 80 percent of the property within the economic zone had been sold or leased. Even so, projections for the final transfer of property to the LRA keep shifting to the future, largely due to environmental cleanup. The Army originally expected to disperse the final acres by 2007. Now that estimate is for 2016.

The LRA is "a twilight organization," said former LRA Director Ylinen "When the last property is sold, the LRA turns the lights out and disappears."

Progress toward fulfilling the economic goals of the LRA has been slow, especially in generating jobs for new employees. "There were false expectations, initially," says current LRA Director Komiskey. But looking at the array of current tenants, she surmises, "I'm not looking for a home run. I'm looking for a lot of base hits. You can win the game that way, too."

Even so, beneath the local optimism lies a persistent worry that maybe, just maybe, the dream will not come together as planned. Will location, government cutbacks for environmental cleanup and wildlife management, and economic competition from the larger nearby communities conspire to scuttle the hard work and vision of environmentalists and developers alike? Chuck Wemstrom, of the Natural Area Guardians, says that he is optimistic, "but those concerns are also blowing in the wind and can be felt out on the prairie. Some days the wind and her song is bittersweet."

And not everyone agrees that the economic and environmental interests are meshing as nicely as it would appear. Some have worried that the igloo technology project may not be as environmentally friendly as perceived, due to the ground disturbance from laying fiber-optic line and the likelihood of frequent visits by technicians. Some worry whether rail-car cleaning will create new environmental problems. And Dan Wenny laments that the best section of prairie is located within the LRA footprint, slated for future development.

And every once in a while, a tempest still flairs. Recently, the LRA wanted to plant a row of austrees, a fast-growing, non-native willow to act as a screen. Environmentalists expressed concerns that the trees will be a new invasive species, quick to spread in the sandy soil. The trees were not planted.

But the general mood is positive that economic and environmental interests can cooperate at the depot. When environmentalists expressed concern several years ago that proposed gyroplane security flights over the server farm (computers in the igloos) would disturb rare birds in the fly zone over the refuge, the plan was nixed. Warren Jackman, himself a member of the Natural Area Guardians, says, "I don't really believe that there ever was an uneasiness between conservation and development interests. It was simply that conservationists were not sure of what economic developers had in mind. What's important is to have an educated dialog going on at all times."

Diane Komiskey sounds a guardedly optimistic note. Economic and environmental interests will mesh, she says, "as long as we each respect one another's territory. I respect their responsibility to protect species and habitat. I would in turn expect them to respect our responsibility to create jobs."

———————————————

My own introduction to the depot occurred in October of 2003. Like many people who grew up within an hour's drive, I had vaguely heard about the depot for most of my life, had read in the newspaper about its closure and about the plans and controversies surrounding its reuse, but had never set foot within these previously heavily-secured grounds. By 2003 the guard house stood empty at the entryway, but chain-link fences and warning signs still kept the public away from all but a few hundred acres that had been cleaned.

October 2003: My wife and I are tagging along with a Natural Area Guardians bird-watching hike on the depot grounds. Most of the group is looking up—at bald eagles, Tennessee warblers, kinglets, turkey vultures, red-tailed hawks, barn swallows, goldfinches, blue jays, and—everyone's favorite—cedar waxwings. A few among the group prefer to look down, at prairie plants. They point out Indian grass with its yellow tint; aster, looking like little white daisies; purplish little bluestem and big bluestem with its trademark turkey foot seedhead; prairie milkweed with pods about to let loose; mullein, a small velvety plant which can be used as a medicinal tea for respiratory problems or—depending on one's needs—as a "poor man's toilet paper." One of the women crushes the leaf of an aromatic sumac to let me smell the mint-like fragrance. But most startling is the prickly pear cactus, unusual in this Midwestern climate but enjoying the sandy soil. The cactus, in October, is fruiting, bearing a grape-sized fruit that one of the women says makes great jelly.

But I can't keep my eyes away from the signs that line the roadway. In a grass field, amid some rail cars: Caution—Contamination Area. On a fence lining the roadway, in faded letters: U.S. Army—Danger: Keep Out. On the door of a deteriorating building, identified to me as the old TNT recovery unit: Danger—Explosives, Keep Away. And again: Restricted Area.

Damnedest wildlife refuge I've ever seen.

Army Headquarters at the Savanna Depot once resided in a stately, though modest, brick building at the top of a small hill, situated next to the parade grounds, across from the depot health clinic and just down the blacktop drive from the commander's and second-in-command's homes and the officers club. "Headquarters" is still spelled out in large silver-colored letters across the front, but from the closure until recently the building was headquarters for the environmental cleanup effort. Now that building is closed, too, and cleanup headquarters has moved elsewhere on the campus.

Shortly after I met John Clarke, BRAC Environmental Coordinator, in his office, he showed me some photos of unexploded ordnance found on the grounds. The items were mortar shells that have lain unexploded since test-firing ceased at the depot six months after its opening in 1918.

But the UXO are just the first of the contaminants. Others are chemical toxins. For example, the buildings where TNT was recovered from obsolete and decaying munitions used to be washed down daily to reduce the risk of accidental explosion, and the resultant raw TNT worked its way into the shallow water table. The TNT "rides like a plume on the water table," says John Rutherford.

Obsolete and decaying munitions of all types were safely detonated or otherwise destroyed in demolition circles. Again, the resultant ash has rendered the soil toxic. At the "old burning grounds," munitions were incinerated and the ashes dumped on an island in the river backwaters. "You can dig there and find ashes ten feet down," says Randy Nÿboer of the Illinois DNR. "Old photos show how the island grew in size due to the buried toxic ash." Debris at the site included 1,578 "live ordnance items," including mortar rounds, grenades, rockets, land mines, projectiles, and fuses.

Next there is the "hand grenade burial pit," one of the more poetically named sites. Or the "Washout Facility" site, where over 67,000 tons of contaminated soil were removed and 10 million gallons of contaminated surface water were treated. At the Fire Training Area 26,000 tons of solvent- and petroleum-contaminated soil were incinerated.

But perhaps the most frustrating toxic site—now cleaned up—is one not in any way connected to the depot mission. In the early 1950s, says Clarke, the U.S. Department of Agriculture (USDA) obtained permission from the Army to bury 860 tons of a banned orchard pesticide (Dinitrolorthocresole, a larvacide) on the depot grounds. The Army dug a trench 250 feet long by 50 feet wide and 20 feet deep, and then hired three local high-school students one summer to slit open the pesticide bags, one by one, and dump them into the trench from the back end of a truck. The three teenagers, covered in pesticide and sweat, ended up in the local hospital with respiratory problems.

This particular site was cleaned in the summer of 2002, the soil removed and taken to an incinerator in Texas. Groundwater testing in subsequent years has shown that the pesticide removal was successful. Over a hundred contamination sites of soil and groundwater have been identified, and a large fan-shaped swath of the depot may potentially harbor UXO, having been within the firing range. Seventy-eight million dollars had been spent on environmental cleanup between 1996 and 2008, says Clarke, and his best-guess estimate is that $150 million more will be required, although the USFWS has pegged the total cost closer to $300 million.

Clarke outlines the cleanup process as follows. First, due to a scarcity of records, the environmental team interviewed former depot employees to identify potential contamination sites. A site investigation follows, and a soil sample is lab-tested. Next, investigators determine the risks posed by a particular site's toxin. If the risk exceeds acceptable parameters, Clarke will do a feasibility study to choose among a variety of alternative remedies for cleaning the site, and finally, execute the cleanup, which may involve excavating the soil, shipping it to an incinerator, and sending it to an EPA-approved landfill. The area is then backfilled with clean topsoil, and prairie grasses planted.

The process for cleaning up UXO begins with a simple walk-through of the surface area, giving the plot a visual sweep and employing geophysical instruments (essentially metal detectors), radar, and sound instruments to detect anomalies underground or on the surface "that could be metallic, explosive, and worth the trouble to dig up." The process, says Clarke, "is less of a science than is cleanup for other contaminants, so it is harder sometimes to get everyone's agreement that a particular parcel is OK." As of summer 2009, most areas of the Depot had been cleaned or deemed free of UXO, but some areas will still need cleanup, according to Clarke.

Environmental cleanup is a slow process. Procedures must be

agreed upon by the federal and Illinois EPA, and communication maintained with the Illinois DNR, the USFWS, and the LRA.

Economic and environmental interests both credit Illinois Congressman Don Manzullo, however, with having created a process that helps move the process forward. Frustrated by slow initial progress and the Army's early reluctance to accept responsibility for cleanup of UXO in particular (which are not considered a superfund waste), Manzullo formed a SMART (Strategic Management Analysis Requirements Technology) Team in August 2000 to help prioritize cleanup sites and to decide "how clean is clean," according to Ed Britton. The SMART team includes members of the Department of Defense, the USFWS, the U.S. and Illinois EPA, as well as some local citizens. According to Britton, "With high ranking members [of each of these groups] on the team, decisions made by the team would stick and not be overturned by persons higher up on the chain of command."

Even so, cleanup efforts are further complicated by the unpredictable availability of funds. "Funding depends on dollars appropriated by Congress and approved by the President," says Clarke, who then points out that the Savanna Depot competes with hundreds of other closed installations, many of which face similar environmental cleanup issues. And, adds Britton, the Homeland Security and Defense Act has put cleanup at the bottom of the list of priorities for the Department of Defense.

An average of $4 million dollars per year has been appropriated since 2004, up from a scant $1 million in 2004. Bit by bit, section by section, the cleanup crawls forward. Site use determines the level of cleanup. Sometimes the Army will issue a Land Use Control (LUC), stipulating that a site has been cleaned to industrial standards and that if future owners want to convert the property to higher levels—a school or residential use, for example—the sellers would be responsible for more intensive cleanup.

The summer of 2008 was shaping up to be a critical year for environmental cleanup and public access, says Ed Britton, as the Army intended to investigate areas alongside the river road that runs almost the length of the property up to a Mississippi overlook. The road lies within the fan-shaped swath of artillery-shelling from the Depot's early days. The overlook has been cleared for the public, but not the areas to the side of the road itself. You can drive to the overlook, but you can't stop along the way. "The Army keeps finding surprises. And they're not good surprises," says Britton, explaining for example that two 75 mm mortar rounds were recently found near the road. Investigation of the river road "will clear—or complicate—so many things," he adds.

Still, Britton predicts the Depot "will never be 100 percent clean. That's the nature of unexploded ordnance."

About once every half hour, a Burlington Northern and Santa Fe train lumbers past the prairie where Dan Wenny and Josh are bird banding. In between, the only sounds are the twitters and trills of grasshopper sparrows, eastern and western meadowlarks—all of which Dan identifies with a keen ear—and the honking of some geese playing in a distant backwater.

There isn't much talking. Dan and Josh are by nature quiet. Josh, the junior from the University of Illinois-Champaign who is majoring in Integrative Biology, came to his interest in birds when he nursed one back to health on his college campus. Wenny holds a Ph.D. in Zoology from the University of Florida, and (at time of this field visit) was the Avian Ecologist for the Illinois Natural History Survey and Director of the Lost Mound Field Station.

Birds are getting caught in the nets now as quickly as Dan and Josh can untangle, measure, and band them. Josh takes a turn untangling the second bird, a male grasshopper sparrow, making slow deliberate moves as if untangling a fishing line. Dan demonstrates how to slip a tiny white band over the bird's leg and dissolve the slit in the plastic with a drop of acetone "so the bird won't snag the band and entangle its leg in something later on."

Dan explains that 75 percent of male grasshopper sparrows are mated and territorial, guarding about a half-acre site. Twenty-five percent are unmated and wander from territory to territory. Birds are mostly monogamous, though unmated males may sneak in from time to time. It is not uncommon to find at least one egg in a nest fertilized by a different male. Male sparrows are territorial and have a slight variation in their songs. A male will listen, then, to see whether its neighbors are within their territories or are encroaching. In the spring, young males will come in and sing in different locations to see whether they'll get chased out.

The third bird entangled is a female, identified by the brood patch on the breast. The female is taken back near to the catch site for release after processing, so she is nearer to her nest.

The fourth is a savanna sparrow, rare here, as this is the southern extremity of its range. Dan invites me to release the bird from the bag when all the measurements are taken.

Fifth is an adolescent red-winged blackbird, not yet possessing the rich red wing markings. The bird is common and is released without banding.

Next, a chipping sparrow, a small bird with a red-brownish head. Dan and Josh search to find a small enough band.

Seventh and eighth, more chipping sparrows. "These will make good practice for Josh," Dan says. One breaks loose from Dan's grasp before he completes measurements.

Ninth, a grasshopper sparrow.

Tenth, a grasshopper sparrow, one already caught and banded earlier this day.

Nets, fishing-tackle box, and catch-and-release. Sort of like sky-fishing.

Lost Mound Refuge—i.e., the 9,715 acres designated for the USFWS subsequent to environmental cleanup—is supposedly named for a mound adjacent to the premises that appeared on early maps and then somehow disappeared from later renditions. Local residents, however, say the name derives from Native American burial mounds on the same hills. But while the name has stuck, no one seems to know for sure its precise derivation.

With 370 additional acres set aside for or already purchased by the Illinois DNR, more than ten thousand acres will be preserved in managed wildlife refuges. Much of the acreage includes Mississippi backwaters and islands, but four thousand of the upland acres are home to Illinois' largest sand prairie.

Ironies abound. The sand prairie made the land less attractive to early pioneers and farmers, which in turn made it more attractive for the Army in 1916 as it scouted land for a proving grounds. When the base closed in early 2000, clean-up costs reduced the pressure to develop larger tracts for economic purposes.

Still, Lost Mound hardly signifies land "lost," forgotten, or abandoned. The refuge harbors forty-seven species of threatened or endangered animals and plants, and includes rare sand prairie, sand savanna, dunes, tallgrass prairie, swamp, marsh, sedge meadow, sand pond, and blowout communities. Most significantly, the refuge contains an unbroken ecological continuum from forested bluffs to prairie to river bottomlands.

The sand prairie itself is an unusual feature in the Midwest, an area more usually known for its dark, rich soil. The sand hills—up to seventy feet deep along the river banks and extending 7.5 miles—resulted from a glacial-melt ice dam located forty miles downstream on the Mississippi near the present day Quad Cities. The ice dam rerouted the river's flow through western Illinois and created a glacial river pool backed up all the way to Savanna. Meltwater entering the glacial pool dropped its sandy sediment formed from bits of rock, ground up by the glaciers scouring across Wisconsin and Minnesota granite. When the ice dam finally broke, the river re-established its course, the pool drained, and great sandy bluffs and river plains were left exposed at Savanna.

Even before the military began its work at the Savanna Depot, early biologists were interested in the special features of the area. In 1908, Dr. Henry Allan Gleason of the Illinois Natural History Survey traveled to the sand prairie to photograph and catalog the landforms, plants, and animal species. His work provides contemporary biologists excellent comparative data. The sand prairie of Gleason's day harbored far fewer trees than at present, says Wenny. The area has lost thirty plant species since the 1908 study. Grasses have declined, while forbs and shrubs, like aromatic sumac, have increased.

A number of factors have caused these changes. Fire, of course, maintains a prairie and keeps the trees at bay. By 1908, and certainly thereafter, there was little contiguous prairie to sustain wildfires, and the Army, for understandable reasons, wanted to minimize the risk of fire in the ammunition storage areas. When cattle were brought in to graze the grasses, particularly around the igloos, one might have expected them to mimic the effects of buffalo, the other great intainers of natural prairie. But, says Wenny, "cattle are wimpy compared to bison, and they seek shade," and as a result they disperse tree seeds through their droppings, leading to more forest encroachment on the prairie.

Cattle produced another significant change on the prairie landscape. Despite the sandy soil, Illinois is a region of tallgrass prairie, but the cattle grazing encouraged short grasses and kept the tall grass species trimmed. When cattle grazing ceased in 1999, tall grasses made a comeback, and bird species counts began to shift back to those Gleason would have observed in 1908. Birds preferring shorter vegetation, including the grasshopper sparrow, western meadowlark, killdeer, horned lark, and vesper sparrow, have declined in recent years. But birds preferring taller vegetation—the bobolink, Henslow's sparrow, dickcissel, northern harrier, and sedge wren—are on the increase.

Discontinuing cattle grazing was a first step in the prairie restoration. But is intervention for the intent of producing a more "natural" prairie itself unnatural? Wenny ponders the question and notes that many prairie fires were actually set by Native Americans to funnel bison into a killing zone and lure others back again when the fresh and luscious grasses re-sprouted.

Even so, the goal of prairie restoration is to re-establish a prairie more like the one observed by Dr. Gleason in 1908. Forest encroachment, for example, has been battled a number of ways, including girdling the bark of trees by cutting a circular swath around the girth to cut off the flow of nutrients between the roots and leaves. Girdled trees were left standing, in the hope that dead trees would provide good roosting places for birds. However, that approach backfired, as the roosting birds actually spread new tree seedlings through their feces. Recent conversations have centered around having a commercial operator bring in a small number of bison to graze the prairie, although the discussions are currently on hold. Fencing for the bison would be a major expenditure for the operator, and with cleanup funding only known on a year-to-year basis, it would be hard to predict what lands will be available. Currently there are no such locations where the bison could be safely viewed by the public, another stumbling block.

Prescribed burns would provide the best prairie maintenance, but that is complicated, due to the UXO. "Explosives and fire don't get along too well," says Randy Nÿboer. But by Spring 2008, the USFWS and Illinois DNR received clearance to burn 945 acres. "We scorched a lot of cedars and locusts encroaching on the grasslands," says Britton.

The prairie and surrounding forest provide excellent habitat for all sorts of species. Two hundred fifty-three bird species have been recorded at Lost Mound, including 128 breeding species, 108 species seen only during spring or fall migration, and 17 species present only in winter.

Lost Mound Refuge is a particularly important haven for the bald eagle, once federally endangered but recently delisted due to a remarkable rebound in population in the past two decades since the banning of the pesticide DDT. By the 1960s, as few as 417 nesting pairs populated the lower 48 states. In recent winters, however, nearly 600 bald eagles have been counted in the Lost Mound Refuge alone, and several year-round nesting sites have been discovered.

Plant species, including a wide range of wildflowers, include the hairy puccoon, Indian grass, June grass, porcupine grass, prairie dandelion, sour dock, little bluestem and big bluestem, prairie milkweed, mullein, aromatic sumac, prairie dropseed, James clammyweed, and, as mentioned before, the most seemingly out-of-place plant in this temperate zone, the common and fragile prickly-pear cactus. Indeed, the fragile prickly-pear is not found in any other location in Illinois.

Lost Mound Refuge is also a cross-roads of species boundaries. It is a southern boundary for northern plants and birds, and a northern boundary for southern species. Eastern and western species overlap here as well. The result is a particularly rich environment of inter-mingled species.

Illinois, like much of the Midwest, was largely a prairie in its natural state, with 22 million grassland acres. Today, only a fraction of a percent of pure prairie remains. Lost Mound Refuge will harbor 4,000 acres of prairie/savanna, though much of it is dotted with warehouses and igloo bunkers. And with a local environmental group, the Prairie Enthusiasts, also buying lands and conservation easements on uplands bordering Lost Mound and restoring those lands to prairie and savanna, a continuous ecosystem from the forested bluffs to the prairie to the river bottomlands will be preserved. Jim Rachuy explains that the area is large enough that "it won't 'leak species.' He explains, "Think of a small island that is a completely natural place, but which has been recently cut off from the mainland. If the island is too small, it will lose species even without human intervention simply because it is too small to maintain a large variety. This is called 'leaking species.' You need a certain size of place in order to maintain the variety of species, and too often a piecemeal approach to preservation doesn't preserve large enough spaces. Lost Mound and its adjacent grounds will be of a large enough size, however, to maintain its rich variety."

The variety of plant and animal species along with the sand prairie terrain makes Lost Mound Refuge particularly rich for scientific study, often by university biologists or their students. One interesting and useful study looked at how prairie restoration techniques can themselves disturb the prairie. According to Ed Britton, there is a stand of red cedars on the refuge that one might have "guessed" should be removed in the interest of sand prairie restoration, but an INHS bird survey showed that the stand is an important roosting site for long-eared owls. "Without this study, we might possibly have taken some 'restoration' action counter-productive to the owls," Britton says.

Environmentalists are excited about Lost Mound's future. They hope to build a migratory bird education center on the grounds. Harry Drucker envisions eco-tourism. A bicycle path may wind through the grounds in the near future. The Prairie Enthusiasts of Northern Illinois, in partnership with the Natural Area Guardians, will soon manage a 200-acre prairie site on the DNR grounds.

According to Dan Wenny, "Lost Mound presents a unique opportunity to combine ecological restoration, biological research, and educational experiences in a way not currently available at any other site." Randy Nÿboer thinks of it in narrative terms. "I want our children's children to be able to see what the land was like when Abraham Lincoln lived in Illinois."

And Nÿboer includes development in his vision for the ideal future. "We have an opportunity to make this a showcase. It takes a lot of effort and money, but I really think we can do it. It depends on people working together who want to preserve *and* develop the land. There is room for both."

Beth Baranksi, a Galena resident who became involved early on as a consultant for the town of Hanover as it tried to recover from the impact of the Depot's closing, describes the Depot as a "Rubik's cube, with lots of faces, and where each face is affected by decisions made by the other sides." Persons involved with economic redevelopment, environmental cleanup, and conservation each have their own vision for the Depot, and sometimes their independent actions can collide with the others', or their individual goals may not carry as much clout as they would in a concerted effort.

In November 2007, the individual sides of the Rubik's cube came together to form the Lost Mound Action Team, with representatives from the LRA, USFWS, Army clean-up force, local conservationists, and other committed individuals. The Action Team, says member Ed Britton, is "trying to tackle problems together rather than individually." The Action Team's current projects include pursuing the introduction of bison onto the prairie; bringing tour buses into specifically approved areas; creating a comprehensive map that will show ownership, UXO, endangered species, and trails, with overlays rather than separate maps for separate purposes; garnering public and political support for the depot plans and activities; gaining public access to as much of the depot as possible; getting volunteer support for projects such as trail-building; establishing a bike trail and a migratory bird education center; and reviewing on a yearly basis the cleanup projects that should receive priority funding. Baranski, an Action Team member, is particularly interested in one of the Team's side-projects to determine whether they can save the Beaty House, an 1840s-era ferry inn that sits in the flood plain and needs to be moved.

"We've been at this for thirteen years," says Britton in regard to the various interests needing to work together. "I think we're getting it down now."

———————————————

By 10 a.m. the mist netting excursion is completed. Dan and Josh carefully slide the nets off the poles, fold, and store them, since a knotted or torn net may cost as much as $75 to replace. I help by pulling out the poles and depositing them in a single location on the prairie, since Dan and Josh will return in a few days for another count.

When we leave, I snap a few photos of the igloos, and imagine computers one day whirring away inside them while grasshopper sparrows go about their business on the prairie.

I take a few detours as I leave the depot. I drive slowly past Headquarters and the parade grounds, past the health clinic and the officers club, past the officers' and the commander's homes, past the machine shops, fire station, and security house, and exit past the squarish indentation in the pavement where the guardhouse once stood.

I never knew these grounds when seven thousand civilians and a thousand Army personnel swarmed about. I never knew the prairie in its natural state or sailed the icy waters of a glacial lake. I never saw artillery fly or trucks dumping toxic loads into gouged trenches, and never felt the sting of panic when the nearby communities realized the loss of jobs. I never saw the exodus of military wares and munitions.

But you can feel it all here, feel it *all*. It's out there, buried, on the prairie. Some of it is toxic, I'll grant you. But much of it, very much, is pure treasures.

Hiking the Driftless:
Lessons in Solitude and Companionship

I

Although I usually hike in the company of my wife, a friend, or a guide, occasionally the hectic pace of daily life calls for a walk in solitude. And while a place called Eden Valley might suggest the biblical Eden's story that "it is not good for man to be alone," today it was very, very good.

It had been several years since I'd hiked Eden Valley, a tiny Clinton County, Iowa, wildlife refuge and campground near the southern edge of the Driftless. The 201-acre county park rises from the valley floor of Bear Creek to hundred-foot bluffs, with hiking trails that wind through forest and meadow.

A central trail leads up from the parking lot past shale outcroppings. The ripples and rushes of Bear Creek below accompany the trail's ascent. Shale soon gives way to overlying limestone boulders that the eons have tumbled down the steep inclines. Interlacing maple roots hold the soil between the boulders.

The central trail erupts into a brilliant meadow at its crest, yellow with compass plants and brown-eyed susans, white with daisies and Queen Anne's lace, and purple with bee balm. Some of the color is in motion, with monarch butterflies flitting about.

At the apex, a forty-foot observation tower overlooks the meadow just slightly above the surrounding forest canopy. Here the solitude is most complete. On the top deck I challenge myself to ten minutes of total silence and stillness, the first five with eyes closed, taking in the sounds of the woods, the occasional car on the road below, the lowing of cattle, and a distant tractor. In the next five I open my eyes, and watch two birds in the canopy and a cloud shaped like Australia, as still and unchanging as a continent.

Deeper into the woods and nestled at the foot of the sheer bluffs are remnants of "Wulf's Den," a relic of the refuge's former life. Arnold Wulf, who sold Eden Valley to Clinton County in 1970, had built a retreat for friends in the 1940s. Today all that is left of the hideaway is a faint line of mortar where Wulf had cemented his lean-to up against the bluff wall, plus a small cavern he'd dynamited for food storage. Above the den are sheer hundred-foot cliffs, as clean as if they'd cleaved just yesterday.

I can agree with Mr. Wulf that Eden Valley would be a great place to bring friends for a laid-back holiday, but today it's equally good for a solitary walk. Thomas Merton, a twentieth-century Trappist Monk from Gethsemane Abbey in Kentucky, wrote of the woods and solitude: "My Zen is in the slow swinging tops of sixteen pine trees." Observe the quiet, he said, and get a feel for the place: "It is important to know where you are put on the face on the earth."

Alone today at Eden Valley, I notice details that would otherwise escape me. A low-slung maple branch catches the one ray of sunlight filtering down to the forest floor. A limb creaking in the wind among the upper branches. The forest succession as maple gives way to walnut and then soon enough to pine, with lower branches barren and dry, stubby and broken.

Scent of pine and sound of silence.

II

Sometimes a memorable hike requires a knowledgeable guide, as I had with Dana Livingston of Dubuque. Livingston, a professor of Spanish at Loras College by profession, is a volunteer at the Mines of Spain Recreation Area near Dubuque, Iowa, who specializes in prairie and savanna restoration.

We rarely passed more than twenty feet without a stop to look at something new.

Our jaunt began on the Prairie Ridge Trail, a twenty-three-acre parcel restored to prairie a decade ago. The parcel had been burned this spring, fire being essential to healthy prairie life since it beats back encroaching woodlands and helps keep invasive plant species in check.

"It's cool to see the way things come back," Dana says, pointing out big bluestem grasses (recognizable by their signature "turkey foot" seed head) capping out at eye level, sunflowers, purple cone-flowers, brown-eyed susans, bee balm, milkweed, and more. Pausing, we catch the drone of insects above a slight wind. The insects, in turn, draw an assortment of birds to add to the overall chatter that is called the stillness of the prairie.

The prairie blooms all summer long, with different plants produc-ing flowers at different points from April through September. "Here, this is what I wanted to show you," Livingston says, pointing out a blazing star whose tiny purple flowers look like punk-rockers' hair.

We wander off the path through the thick of the prairie. He points out a compass plant, its leaves aligned roughly north to south. Every twenty feet there is something different, and we stop frequently to consult the laminated wildflower booklet Dana carries in his pocket: white wild indigo, mountain mint, little bluestem grass, Indian grass, St. Johns wort, goldenrod, Queen Anne's lace with its carroty root.

We come upon a five-lobed yellow flower that we can't identify. Out comes the booklet. Partridge pea, we decide, checking the hint of a reddish center and the march of dainty leaves. We swish further through the grasses. Dana waves a stand of Indian grass back and forth on the prairie floor. "Isn't it a beaut?" he says.

Eventually we cross into a more recently recovered prairie on the Cedar Ridge Trail. In its third year since having been replanted from farmland to prairie, it is not yet as lush and diversified as the older stand. It takes a while. In a prairie there is as much going on under-neath the soil as above, with a thick mat of plant roots enmeshing with a special mix of soil bacteria. "Some experts think it may take a couple hundred years to fully reestablish a prairie," says Livingston.

Part of this newer stand was previously a hayfield, and the old grazing grasses are still competing with the natural grasses.

But what is a natural prairie? Out in the expanse, our conversation broadens. How much of the old prairie fire ever was "natural"—as in lightning-induced—and how much was set by Native Americans who knew that the vibrant grasses that rejuvenate after a fire would draw bison and other prey? Native Americans also used prairie fire as a tool to drive bison into hunting traps.

And is it more "natural" today to keep our hands off the prairie and let the woodlands encroach, as they will, or to set controlled burns to mimic the prairie fires of long ago?

Such questions dissipate, however, when there is work to be done, and our hike next brings us to Dana's own pet project, the edge of the woods where he has been restoring a transitional savanna. Savannas occurred in areas like Dubuque where the bluffland woods gave way to the western prairie. In the transitional places, the grassland was dotted with broad-limbed oaks and other hardwoods.

The prairie is subtle, we agree on our hike back. In the American West, mountains trumpet their majesty, and even our Mississippi woodlands and bluffs tower above us. Beauty in such cases seems to dwarf us mere mortals by comparison.

But on the prairie, often overlooked as plain, the majesty is eye-level, even underfoot, in a diminutive purple blazing star or a tuft of big bluestem.

III

If you're going to hike the Eagle Scout Trail at the Mines of Spain, bring along plenty of conversation. You'll be out there a while. But bring along an appreciation for silence, too. You'll want both.

My wife Dianne and I hike the Eagle Scout Trail a couple of times a year, catching the seasons as they unfold if we can.

We are talking, always talking. The day, our jobs, our kids, our plans. Our words gather in the hollow and flow through the stream bed.

A half mile from the parking lot, the valley narrows between ledges of exposed and tumbled limestone. We are suddenly quiet. If there are words at all, they are memories—of Cub Scout boys, years ago, climbing all over these rocks that arise from the valley floor like a spine of earth-bone.

On again, we cross the creek bottom now on stepping stones and begin the first ascent. Silence would be good now, saving some air for breath as the trail climbs steeply out of the valley toward Mississippi blufftops. First, though, we stop briefly to take in a patch of white birch bark against a baby blue sky.

Our hike and conversations take us next to the site of a now-razed farm, known as the Wiederholt place. Dianne and I reconstruct the layout of the farm, tracing the foundations of barn, house, and shed that are sinking back into the landscape. Here we find a toppled chimney. Over there the cellar stairs. The only remaining structure is a cattle barn that leaks in rain, wind, and light.

Soon enough we are back walking. Once or twice we have encountered other hikers, but usually not. We talk about everything. We talk through the woods, through bends in the trail, down ravines and back up the other sides. Somewhere along the trail—in woods and prairie—are three lead-mine shafts and Native American burial mounds. They do not announce themselves, and to date we have not seen them.

We talk until we emerge onto the first of three blufftop prairies. In all, about sixteen acres of prairie have been restored from tilled farmland along the trail route. Here—depending on the season—the heat or cold intensifies and the wind blows away all talk. From here the view is expansive, up and down the Mississippi River. A short diversion on a side-footpath ends in a thick cedar woods on a narrow fingerling bluff immediately above the river. Always the river, silently below. We stop for a while, just taking it in. No one has been here for a while, we just know it. The place is not used to human-talk.

But we are not used to long silences. We return to the main trail and hike through the remaining prairies until the trail loops back on itself and sends us back homeward.

It's been a good afternoon. We've told the land something about human-folk through our long conversations. In return, the land has taught us something about silence.

IV

"The great thing about snowshoes," I said to my wife last winter when the snow got too deep for cross-country skiing, "is that I can be outside in even more miserable weather." With that I strapped on a pair of aluminum snowshoes and headed out alone onto the golf course behind my house in the aftermath of a snow-and-ice-storm, when the sky had cleared to reveal a brilliant full moon. As I emerged up out of a wooded valley path, the snowshoe crampons gripping down against the icy mix, I came upon a stand of twisted oaks at the edge of the clearing. Below me, the shadows of the gnarled branches snaked out across the snow, as clear and sharp as the real branches stretched out against the night sky overhead. Above me—or, more precisely, between the full moon and myself—the slight icing on the branches sparkled like white Christmas lights. It was a magical night, and one that I would have missed if I hadn't strapped on the shoes.

I wouldn't say that snowshoeing is my favorite method of win-tertime mobility. Give me the quick, soft glide of cross-country skis across a whispery powder of snow. Give me a hike in the woods when the snow cover is thin or the ground barren and hard. Then I'll glide easily over the hills, checking out exposed limestone boulders and the ebb and swell of land.

Snowshoeing, by contrast, is hard work with its deliberate lift-ing and lowering of each shoe, time and again, across a deep snow. It can be plodding and labored. I recently came home from an outing drenched in sweat, thinking there has to be some payoff for a recre-ation like this.

But then time melts, and I place myself back at my first solo hike with the snowshoes last winter at Lost Canyon. I've heard about an Ice Cave there, and I want to see it. Not knowing exactly where it might be, I guess that I have found it when I see hoarfrost tingeing the bluff face, a triangular white froth above the dark maw where the cave breathes. From a slight distance, I hear a sound within—water dripping into an interior pool, a persistent, regular, echoing plink. A hint of ice formations—just visible from the path—huddle at the opening.

Drawing near, I find just inside the mouth of the cave a hundred two-foot-tall ice figurines formed from the slow dripping and freezing of water. A hoard of tiny persons, encased in the icy sheen. Slender, wet, curvaceous. Slumped, sorrowing, prayerful. Stooped shoulders, faceless heads. Save one—here, in front, a dripping figure with skeletal eyes and jaw, shrouded in a Biblical robe. There, an angel humped with frozen wings. Frozen monks in silent praise. Huddled masses, milling in place. Merlin entrapped.

Faeries must hide here, painting hoarfrost on the rock face to lure strangers to the interior pool where water drips with a persistent, regular, echoing plink.

Without the snowshoes, I never would have seen it.

V
But solitude seared it onto the landscape of memory.

The Mountain That Soaks
in the Water

A mist rolls out over the Mississippi River this morning. In the foggy distance, a miniature island mountain, cut off on either side from the river bluffs that trumpet the Wisconsin and Minnesota shorelines, rises 400 feet from waterline to topmost crag.

To the Sioux it was "Pah-hah-dah," or the Mountain separated by water. For the Winnebago, "Hay-nee-ah-chah," the Soaking Mountain. The French called it "La Montagne qui Trempe dans l'Eau," or Trempealeau, The Mountain that Soaks in the Water. Native American legend hails that spirits whisked it away from upriver during a storm and placed it here to save its sacred burial grounds.

This big old rock, the mists, legends, the bluffs lining either shore, and the Father of Waters rolling beneath, all have me pondering. But all I know is that, when the mist burns off, it's a glorious October day, and the thousands of ducks and geese rendezvousing at Trempealeau's foot prior to their southward migration are splashing away like it's the last day at the city pool. It's an old, old mountain, and the day is new, and therein lies the central paradox.

Trempealeau Mountain is located about thirty miles northwest of La Crosse, Wisconsin, in Perrot State Park. The island and park are contiguous with the Trempealeau National Wildlife Refuge, an engineered wetlands and backwaters that is home and host to hundreds of aquatic species and migrating fowl.

Dianne and I first found Trempealeau Mountain the previous spring while searching for new bicycle trails an overnight camping trip distance away from our home along the Mississippi River in Dubuque, Iowa. The map took us three hours upriver to La Crosse and slightly beyond to the town of Trempealeau (pop. 1,650), to Perrot State Park and the Trempealeau National Wildlife Refuge, and to the Great River State Trail where we biked forty miles on a converted railway bed.

Then the rain set in overnight, and in the next morning's dampness we hiked the Brady's Bluff Trail through a fern-laden woods, past forty-foot Saint Petersburg Sandstone tower formations, alongside and sometimes across moss-covered logs fallen and decaying along the path. The trail twists time and again along the hillsides, upward through the eons where sandstone outcroppings give way to blasts of shale, all formed in a succession of ancient seas. The sea floor uplifted and fell, time and again, until finally rising above ocean level for the last time 230 million years ago.

The trail lopes upward, the final ascent made easier by stone- and then treated-lumber stairways, topping out at a Hopewellian Native American burial mound at a 520-foot overlook, where we saw Trempealeau Mountain awash in a river of mist.

Always a mist. What is it trying to hide?

This is the river of great bluffs. Up and down the river as far as the eye can see on clearer days, 400- to 500-foot forested bluffs line the shore on either side, each cut sharply and steeply by the ravines of past and present creek beds. Downstream, Lock & Dam #6 pools the Mississippi waters across the entire valley floor; upstream, the Trempealeau National Wildlife Refuge spreads out in a marshy expanse.

The river that cut this valley once raged nearly blufftop to blufftop as meltdown from the last great glacier twelve thousand years ago coursed through the Driftless Land. The meltwater ran deep and furious. Some river slopes at Trempealeau harbor sand beds 200 feet above the current water level, dropped there when the river began to recede. And the river bottom was deeper as well, as the present-day river bed sits atop an alluvial base of glacial till 150 feet deep.

The coursing river was restless and powerful. Trempealeau Mountain may once have been connected to the tall bluffs on the Minnesota shore, but then the river shifted south and west, slicing off Trempealeau Mountain. With the Trempealeau River still feeding the northeast corner of the bluff, Trempealeau Mountain became an island, just one of three such rock-mountains in the entire run of the Mississippi.

Unless, of course, it was whisked here by spirits.

I returned to Trempealeau by myself in October. The bluffs looked bluish-green amid a general mist. A train passed quickly and quietly at the foot of the bluffs on the Minnesota shore. The town of Winona basked at their feet.

On this October morning, Trempealeau Mountain arises from the mid-river mist and announces its sleepy, wooded self. But it does not easily reveal its secrets.

In some respects, Trempealeau readily gives up its history.

A monument inside Perrot State Park marks the 1685–86 winter encampment of Nicholas Perrot, a French fur trader and emissary to Native Americans of the French-claimed Midwest. When Perrot and his men found themselves iced in on their trek up the Mississippi, they chose a spot "at the foot of the mountain which sheltered them from some of the winter's cold and behind them was a great prairie abounding in wild beasts," as one of Perrot's men noted in his journal. More than three hundred years later, in 1996, high-school students on an archaeological dig found what is believed to be Perrot's winter-time garbage pit, containing the bones of bear, deer, buffalo, elk, and raccoon.

Perrot gathered furs over winter and headed north in the spring to cash in. By 1689, Perrot had claimed the land west of the Great Lakes and east of the Rocky Mountains for France. His post at Trempealeau lingered for a few years after his departure, and then the land sunk back again into solitude and obscurity.

In 1731 the French tried again, establishing a post almost on the same grounds, with René Godefroy sieur de Linctot in charge. A series of commandants and post abandonments and reoccupations took place until the French relinquished their control to the British in 1763.

British and American explorers frequently noted the exceptional mountain arising from the river. Jonathan Carver, exploring for England in the 1760s, described "a mountain remarkably situated, for it stands by itself in the middle of the river, and looks as if it had slidden from the adjacent shore into the stream." American explorer Henry Rowe Schoolcraft in 1820 wrote of "an isolated mountain of singular appearance [that] arises out of the center of the river, to a height of four or five hundred feet, where it terminates in crumbling peaks of naked stone."

The British ceded the area to the United States when the War of Independence ended (although it would take two more generations for the U.S. to wrest it from its Native American inhabitants). When the U.S. established Fort Snelling near Minneapolis in 1819, traffic up and down the Mississippi increased, and the intermittent posts that had occasionally popped up near Trempealeau Mountain eventually formalized into the town of Trempealeau in 1851.

The Trempealeau Hotel, now the Trempealeau Hotel Café, dates back to 1871. On this October day almost a century and a half later, I am sitting here at a small, plain table near the windows, watching the river roll by some forty yards away, awaiting arrival of a burger and fries, and sipping on a Spotted Cow beer (a tough choice between this and the Fat Squirrel).

History reveals itself in the oddest places. The back of the menu sports an excerpt from a local author's book, *Trempealeau Mountain*, written by George Henry Willett in 1914:

> [Robert] Burns sung the praises of Bonnie Doon—because the Doon was the river he knew best; had he lived in our village he would have sung the beauties of the Mississippi, and his song would have been as sweet. . . . The poet sings the beauty that he finds next at hand—and Walden Pond will do as well as the Atlantic.

Finally, as I finish lunch, the clouds lift. I'll save this pondering for another day. The October sun and the Spotted Cow have finally decided what kind of day it is going to be, and I am fine with that.

After lunch at the café, I pull in at the Trempealeau National Wildlife Refuge. The honking just beyond the parking lot isn't from cars, however, but from the geese and ducks gathered in hordes in the backwaters. The refuge, with its elaborate system of dikes and pumps, harbors restored wetlands that serve as waterfowl migration gathering sites. Ducks and geese by the thousands stop and refuel on their way south for the winter and their return migration in the spring.

It sounds like the city pool as I near the observation deck, a general ruckus of diving and splashing. There are probably fifty ducks immediately before me, thousands in the wide sweep of refuge backwater. When I approach the edge of the deck, about twenty ducks rev off in foot-dragging flight—a rush of wings and splash—and settle back down about thirty feet away.

Twenty geese are passing overhead in a small V heading south; ten are in formation heading north, practicing flight patterns in anticipation of the long haul, and then regrouping at the waterfowl bar and grill.

I identify several of the species listed on the information board: Canvasback (white body, red neck), Scamp (black head, white beak), Goldeneye (white breast, black head, white cheek), Redhead (red top and white beak), Bufflehead (smallish, with white and black head), Ringnecked (red eye, white beak with a black tip). There are Puddle Ducks (the city pool again) who like the shallow water, Blue-winged Teal, Pintail, Gadwall, Mallard, Green-winged Teal, Shoveler, Wood Ducks, Wigeons. In the distance I see what I initially take to be dried-up water lilies, but a peek through my binoculars reveals that they are hundreds more ducks and geese, lollygagging in the backwaters. The migrating waterfowl have collected after the first leg of their journeys from all around the upper Midwest. They feed on fish, fingernail clams, and plant roots before resuming their southward trek.

The refuge dates back to 1936, when it was established with 700 upland acres above the river level. Acquisitions and land trades have brought the Trempealeau National Wildlife Refuge to 6,226 acres, about 4,000 of which are wetlands.

The natural river, before the construction of the Mississippi dams, would dramatically rise and fall through the seasons, flooding wetlands and then leaving them to dry out, a cycling of wet and dry that was perfect for habitat. While the dams created wetlands, the pools are too constantly wet and too mired in silt for effective habitat. An engineering project completed in 1999 has enhanced these above-the-dam wetlands at Trempealeau with more than three miles of dikes, gates, and water pumps dividing the refuge into five pools. The dikes and pumps at the refuge mimic the natural river's cycles. Every couple of years, the Refuge technicians drastically drop the water level in the summer, allowing for more growth of aquatic vegetation on the receding shores and mud flats. When the water level is raised again in the fall, the ducks and geese have drive-up food service as they paddle amid the newly-flooded vegetation.

In the year 2000, refuge technicians drained down and then re-flooded the pools. Waterfowl counts indicate a huge success: in 1999, 5,600 ducks and 570 geese were counted by local volunteers; in 2000, the numbers had jumped to 27,000 ducks and 2,100 geese.

In the fall, migration patterns vary by species and by year. "One week," says Park Ranger Jennifer Lilla, "we might have a bunch of ruddy ducks, and the next week the canvasbacks have flown in," depending on food supply and weather from wherever they've flown. In the spring there are shorter visits by returning ducks and geese. "It's more of a place to stop and rest their wings."

Other wildlife in the Refuge includes "60 mammal species, 250 species of birds, 30 species of reptiles and amphibians, and 25 fishes," according to the Refuge website; "In October, as many as 8,000 cormorants and 2,000 white pelicans feed and stage for their flight south." In recent years, observers have counted as many as 138 bald eagles on a single day.

That's a lot of kids rollicking at the pool.

Just out of earshot of the honking wetlands lies another altogether different ecosystem of the Trempealeau National Wildlife Refuge, a sand prairie that rolls in gentle swells on a bottomland ledge above the river level. Laid down by an old path of the Trempealeau River, the deposited sand was blown into dunes by winds pummeling over the nearby glaciers twelve thousand years ago.

Through the years, the dunes oscillated between prairie and forest-cover, and frequently found middle ground in oak-prairie savanna.

After the Winnebago and Dakota ceded the land east of the Mississippi in 1837, the prairie began losing the fight against the forest and the plow. When the Refuge was established in 1936, the sand dunes were largely wooded. But an oak blight took its toll on the forest in the 1980s, and after burning the infected trees, the Park Service began efforts to re-establish the prairie. Today a walk through the prairie offers a display of Indian grass, switch grass, big and little bluestem, prairie dropseed, and more.

Under the soil, the prairie is active as well. Prairie grasses set down root networks as deep and wide as the visible plants; these roots hold the wind-blown soil in place, absorb rainwater like sponges, and protect the grasses against drought and fire.

Many hillsides on the Trempealeau prairie are graced with oak savannas, and small oaks at the periphery are evidence of continual forest encroachment. To combat encroachment, says Ranger Lilla, Refuge officials try to burn all areas in a rotation of three to five years, but the cycle depends on manpower, weather conditions, and the lay of the landscape. Lilla shows me a section burned the prior year; the only remaining evidence among the tall grasses is some charred tree stumps. Lilla points out the location for the upcoming spring's burn, where three-foot oaks are trying to take over, but the site will be a difficult one with a hillier terrain and full-grown oaks that need to be spared.

It is January before I can return to the Trempealeau Refuge. The sky is a big, pale blue, the air icy, sharp, and clear. Ice chokes the tree

stumps and shoreline grasses of the backwaters. Any ducks left behind would have frozen solid to the river. There is no sound, save the
wind and occasional winter bird. The city pool is closed.

Now that public events at the Refuge have taken a short, winter-
time lull, Ranger Lilla drives me through the Refuge, beaming with
wonder and pride. "You can come here any season," she says, "and
experience something unique. It could be a barn owl, a fox loping
across the road, you just never know." Now I learn how Refuge officials lower and raise water levels in the several backwater pools
in order to keep shoreline habitat healthy for waterfowl. She shows
me the water control structures, some merely mechanical gates that
keep water out or let water in, some involving pumps and bilges. She
drives me through the sand prairie, pointing out last year's burn and
the encroaching oaks on a hillside. She shows me a sunken foundation and steps, all that remain of a prairie farmstead from before
1936. Tells me about the bald eagle counts from the winter, points out
an eagle's nest in a nearby tree. Lilla likes to be out in the winter: "It's
like an open window, you have the chance to see into the trees, to see
the forest floor."

It seems like a lazy day. Most birds have flown south. Trees and
grasses and the river itself are waiting out the long, deep freeze. On
the way home, I stop to take pictures of a silent, frozen lake.

And out in the river, Trempealeau Mountain still waits, its story
locked in the ice-cold rock.

Who are these spirits that legend says moved Trempealeau Mountain from its home ninety miles upstream? Why plunk it down right
here? Who created the legend, and why do I insist on calling it legend?

These are among the questions swirling in the mist and blowing
in the icy, cold breeze on the days I have visited Trempealeau.

The oldest human artifact discovered near Trempealeau is a

ten-thousand-year-old notched stone, meaning that the region was inhabited near the end of the last glacial period. Hopewell Culture burial mounds—in the park, on the mountain, near the town, and in surrounding regions—date from 100 BC to 500 AD, although many have been lost or desecrated due to excavation, cultivation, ransacking, and erosion.

A minor squall erupted in the town of Trempealeau a few years ago, according to author Laurie Hovell McMillin in her book *Buried Indians*, when local residents took exception to archaeologists' claims that rare platform mounds grace the bluff above the town. Platform mounds—burial or ceremonial mounds with a sheered, flat top—might suggest a Native American village outpost linked to the Cahokia culture that thrived in a city of 10,000-20,000 people near the present location of St. Louis around 1100 AD.

But the Trempealeau residents weren't buying it. They'd been burned before, when they learned that Perrot State Park officials back in the 1930s had constructed some artificial mounds to replace authentic ones destroyed for beach access and outhouses. How could they trust that these newly discovered mounds were for real? Besides, the town's old-timers insisted that they would have known if there were true mounds "up there." Residents worried what financial responsibilities they might incur for upkeep if the mounds were authentic. To date, the town council has resisted efforts by the Archaeological Conservancy to preserve the mounds.

Meanwhile, Trempealeau Mountain itself quietly harbors effigy mounds up to forty feet long in the shape of birds, deer, and dogs.

The ages passed. The years cycled through a familiar landscape of seasons:
- First Bear Month
- Last Bear Month
- Raccoon Breeding Month
- Fish Become Visible Month
- Drying-of-the-Earth Month
- Digging Month
- Cultivating Month

- Tasseling Month
- Elk Whistling Month
- When the Deer Paw the Earth Month
- Deer Breeding Month
- When the Deer Shed Their Horns Month

Historians originally believed that the mound-builders disappeared from the Midwest landscape somewhere around 1200 AD. But more recent scholarship suggests that the Woodland people may simply have been the ancestors of natives that European explorers met when first entering the region: the Oneota and Ioway, and—in the locale of Trempealeau—the Sioux and Winnebago (or Ho-Chunk).

The Winnebago migrated to the La Crosse area from the Great Lakes in 1787, led by Chief Buzzard Decorah. Their descendants spread up and down the river, but Buzzard's son One-Eyed Decorah found his favorite hunting grounds in the prairie north of Trempealeau. Rivalries intensified among tribes seeking hunting grounds and village sites grown increasingly scarce due restrictive land treaties and the press of American settlers arriving in droves. One-Eyed Decorah played a key role in ending the Black Hawk War that had raged just to the south when he delivered Black Hawk to the U.S. Army in 1832.

In less than a decade, One-Eyed Decorah's help in capturing Black Hawk would be forgotten by the Americans. In 1837 Decorah signed a treaty removing the Winnebago from the eastern shore of the Mississippi.

Trempealeau Mountain stayed on. The sacred spirits who made their home on the blufftop were unknown to the new white settlers.

I first saw Trempealeau Mountain from Brady's Bluff in Perrot State Park. Rising from the misty river that day and on subsequent visits, it looked as if it were shrouded in a secret that I might learn if I could be still long enough.

But in the end, it is muteness that I hear mostly, the muteness of rock, the silent earth bones. Ancient seas, come and gone. Uplift and glacial melt. Mound-builders' culture dissipated into the wind. Nicholas Perrot on a brief winter's stay, and the French come and gone. The Winnebago driven off. Settlers, oblivious to the past, laying down a new culture, themselves now dead and forgotten. Visitors who come and go. Migratory ducks and geese, each spring and fall, come and gone.

Even Trempealeau Mountain is under siege. The Trempealeau River that feeds the bay that washes the feet of the great bluff on the eastern side of the Mississippi each year fills a little more with sediment. Soon only its western foot will bathe in water.

Mountains ride out the eons, but not eternity. What do spirits do when the mountains, hills, and plains that nurtured them pass away?

I think that this is what Trempealeau Mountain is contemplating in the mist. If it knows the answer, it is not yet giving it up.

Autumn Here

*Cold clouds flying, trees half bare, wet
leaves lying around everywhere, the broad
valley beautiful and lovely. The wonderful, mysterious, lonely sense of an autumn
evening.*

—Thomas Merton,
Dancing in the Water of Life

A few trees have already blazed and dropped their leaves, but most
of them are, like me, stubbornly clinging to summer. This first week
of October has been unseasonably warm—about 20 degrees above
the usual average daily highs. As summer rolls into fall, you can easily forget that the warm spell is fleeting. The grass keeps growing with
a vengeance. My pepper plants keep bearing with no sign of letting
up. I don't know whether to bask and rejoice, or to worry whether
this is another sign of global warming. Let me think about that on yet
another bike ride.

But the signs of fall are here. The poplar tree in my backyard is
among the first to lose its leaves, littering the grass on a daily basis.
The neighborhood trees are abuzz with hidden sparrows anxious
with flight plans. They practice the art of flocking, swooping across
streets and fields, not yet heading south, but gathering and getting
everyone in a general ruckus. Virginia Woolf aptly described flocking rooks as "a vast net with thousands of black knots in it . . . cast up
into the air; which, after a few moments sank slowly down upon the

trees." I've seen small contingents of ducks and geese alighting across the sky, not yet heading south but en route to a gathering place.

Soon enough the maples will blaze orange and yellow. They'll shed their blood-red October leaves. The oaks will just turn brown. On cold October mornings as I drive to school, big patches of sky will be dotted and flowing with flocking birds.

There is much to do before the season ends.

I'm within striking distance of 3,000 miles on my bicycle odometer. A few more Saturday mornings in southwest Wisconsin along the river and up into the bluff roads should suffice, along with scratching out as many after-work, half-hour crankings through the steepest hills of the Mines of Spain. The real race is against the whittling daylight hours.

The pale blue sky of a warm November afternoon speaks of urgency. On a hike through the Mines of Spain, Dianne and I climb a trail from the valley floor up into the bluff, prowl around some scraggly pines—dry and scratchy as the rubbly ground they claw up from—and turn a glorious corner into a stand of birch. The white bark and yellowing leaves are etched against the blue sky, and you can feel in your bones that this is the last warm Sunday of the season.

Canoe excursions have also taken on the urgency of "one last time" to our favorite local launches. Today we put in at Massey Station, a county park, campground, and marina just south of Dubuque. Noting a steady north wind and a healthy current after the wet fall, we change our usual path and paddle north, upstream, working hard at the outset so we can drift back downstream on the way back. We usually avoid the river channel, but there's no alternative in this direction, so we hug the shoreline for a quick exit should it be necessary. But much of the shoreline is bluff—a ledge of fine-layered, crumbling shale beneath the railroad tracks, and an expanse of limestone and woods above. The mid-afternoon autumn sun finds a peculiar slant through the forest and onto the river. We talk and we don't talk, wearing the day comfortably.

———————————

I love all seasons here in the Driftless Land. Unlike my neighbors, I will hope for a snow-gorged winter with burst after burst of six- and ten-inch snowfalls so I can rev up the snowblower and make clean slices through the driveway and sidewalk before heading out to the golf course on cross country skis. And who doesn't like spring? Once, on a March morning before dawn as I took the dog out to the backyard, I could actually hear earthworms churning in the soil after a thawing rain, an earthy, lusty, unsettling sound of the world reawakening. But then give me a hot, barefoot summer day, one with plenty of sweat and steep hills to be tackled by bicycle. And autumn is the time for a hike in the woods, the sun warm and the air cool, the world dried out and readied for winter. I don't dread autumn's slide toward winter. But I can understand what Gretel Ehrlich meant when she wrote that the Japanese word for autumn means "beauty tinged with sadness." No, it's not the coming cold and snow that I dread; it's knowing that the earth will be brown for months on end. Snow in this globally-warmed region is intermittent, softening the landscape when it falls, but winter thaws bring back a deadly beige. Green won't return until April.

I've wondered sometimes what precise emotion I feel when I see those long V-formations of ducks and geese flying south along the Mississippi, or the even larger flocks of smaller birds swooping from one horizon to the other, looking altogether like a floating connect-the-dots puzzle. One October morning while driving to work some years ago it became clear to me: what I feel is the strange sense of being left behind.

True, we humans won't be alone here as a species. The blue jays will stay all winter, as will a smattering of other toughened birds. The bald eagles will descend from up north and make this their winter home. Field mice will poke out of the snow on occasion, looking for grain. Almost every trek in the woods will be graced by the sighting of deer, revealed by the flick of a white tail among the leaf-barren branches.

But even though I know that not all creatures are migrating or bundling up in some cave for hibernation, when I look up at the urgent flocks heading south, it feels like we humans have been left here for winter as the sole stewards. In general, I don't know that we are up for the task. But no one has bothered to ask, and here we are as the last days of autumn whittle down.

Once, several years ago, I went camping and bicycling in early November along the Root River in southeast Minnesota with my son's Boy Scout troop. The weather turned cold and wet when we hunkered down for the night, and I decided that the back of my pickup—with its aluminum topper—would be drier, if not warmer, than a night in the tent. With nightfall, the rain turned over to thick, white clumps of snow falling fatly, so dense I could hear their muffled plumps on the aluminum roof, drumming out the last faint graces of autumn.

Manitoumie. Sinsinawa.

I

Manitoumie. The Great Spirit dwells there.

The wind is chilled on this December morning. The sky, tenuously linking the states of Iowa, Wisconsin, and Illinois at their Mississippi River conjunction, is an icy pale blue. It sharpens the mind.

The view from where I live on the Iowa bluff dips first across downtown Dubuque and then stretches across the ice-covered river. Then scales the river bluffs on the Wisconsin shore. You can scan north to the wide sweeping curve where the Mississippi takes a pronounced east-west shift. You can scan south to Illinois. But your eye will catch, focus, and return to the great mound rising, pronounced, some three hundred feet above southwest Wisconsin's rolling hills.

The mound will focus your view from every direction. You will see it twenty, thirty miles away, from both sides of the Mississippi, a key signature feature of the local landscape.

Sinsinawa Mound. The name, deriving from the Mesquakie (the last Native American tribe to occupy the region), means "the young eagle." But the Mesquakie called the whole local region of Southwest Wisconsin "Manitoumie." The land where the Great Spirit dwells.

II

Today, Sinsinawa Mound is home or national center to 600 Sinsinawa Dominican Catholic sisters across the U.S. and in foreign missions. In addition, the Sinsinawa complex, comprising 450 acres, offers retreat and educational programs, advocates for social justice, hosts a local theater group, serves as a retirement home for sisters, and more. The progressive thinking of the Dominicans is reflected in the modernistic round chapel, the focus on women's spirituality in programs and in the bookstore, and on the attention and care given to social issues.

But these are the trappings, the outward manifestations, of sacred land. What you see is the fruit of a productive soil. Beneath it lies a solid and indestructible bedrock, unchanged for millennia, whatever the current shape of the surface activity.

For the Great Spirit dwells here.

III

Manitoumie's first spirits coalesced from the decay of shelled sea creatures in a primordial Ordovician sea 450 million years ago. A great warm and shallow sea washed over most of America's Midwest, and the shells of sea creatures—brachiopods, cephalopods, and gastropods—piled thickly onto the ocean floor, packed in sediment. The weight of years and the heat of subterranean forces pressed these into a thick layer of Galena dolomite limestone, the lime pressed and transformed from the shells.

The continental plates, adrift on the earth's mantle like slow suds in a bathtub, pushed and heaved, and for a while the land uplifted and the seas rolled back. Then the land dipped beneath another sea, and rose and fell again, as new layers of bedrock were laid down—a scaly Maquoketa shale and another limestone called Niagara dolomite.

The land heaved another time, the seas rolled back, and vegetation sprang up and formed a thick soil atop the bedrock. Eons later, glacial icepacks bore down across the mid-continent from the north, advancing and retreating many times as the climate alternately cooled and warmed.

The last great glacial period, the Wisconsin, butted up against the edge of human memory twelve thousand years ago, but never reached southwest Wisconsin and the surrounding region. Land at the glacier's edge, however, was eroded for centuries by meltwater when the warming began, resulting in great bluffs rising mightily from the Mississippi and steep, rounded fingers of woodland sharply etched by tumbling ravines.

And topping these hills are the great mounds of southwest Wisconsin. Their topmost layer of Niagara dolomite once covered the entire region from here to the Great Lakes, but to the north the glaciers overlaid the Niagara with thick layers of drift and blown-in loess. In the Driftless Land, the surface Niagara was undercut by the crumbling, easily erodible shale beneath, until bit by bit only scattered mounds of Niagara remained intact. Today, four great mounds grace the southwestern Wisconsin landscape—Platteville Mound, Belmont, Blue Mound, and Sinsinawa.

I imagine the Great Spirit moving with slow and studied stewardship among the four great mounds, and coming finally to Sinsinawa Mound, closest in proximity to the Mississippi, Father of Waters. For this would be a fine place in which to dwell.

Manitoumie.

IV

It is 9:15 on a late-summer morning. The dew at the base of Sinsinawa Mound lies thick on the grassy paths that lead upward through the woods, and it soaks the tips of my boots. Already the air is becoming humid. Locusts whine in the treetops where the woods bear a thickness of green. In the soft soil there is damp decay. A white, puffball mushroom the shape and size of a doughy bread loaf squats at the base of an oak, just inches beyond the path. The path leads upward.

I find a great slanted limestone boulder about 10 feet wide and 12 feet long partway up the hill, and climb it for a better view of the lowlands. Moss clings to its northern face, and clumps of grass have sprouted on its pockmarked surface. I know that these blocks have tumbled from above, but the thick mats of soil and grass make it look as if the boulders have just now awakened and heaved upward from the bedrock, tearing and ripping tufts of dirt, leaves, and under growth from the forest floor in the ascent.

Scrabbling back down the slanted boulder, I return again to the path, noting my footprints in the soft humus beyond the trail. No one has been here for a while.

The tell-tale shale lies halfway up the mound, at the lip of a wide ravine. For a while I pick among the loosened rock, looking for fossils, but I come up empty-handed, except for an agate, which I slide into my jeans pocket like a talisman. The shale is cool to my palm, somewhat moist, and crumbles like a cookie.

There are, in fact, several paths that lead upward through the woods, and they all converge at the top of the Mound. And here, like the balding pate of an old man, lies a grassy, bulldozed mini-mound upon the Mound, an access point for a water reservoir that serves the complex of Dominican sisters who reside at the base of the hill. The view from here is expansive: farm fields stretching away, country roads accenting the rolling hills, the distant bluffs, and an etched dark stripe where the river hides.

Others, of course, have been here long ago. On the sun-bleached, red, wooden, reservoir shed, dozens of long-ago visitors have carved their names or initials, perhaps teenaged girls who once attended the Dominican high-school academy, or young sisters in some small act of defiance:

- HJD 1925
- Mar 8, 1904—M.J. Owl
- MJO Mar 17, 1904
- Leveta Roling, Oct 1919
- J.C. Booth,'08

Many spirits.

When I return down the path, the puffball mushroom has broken from its mooring and tumbled down the slope and onto the trail. The bedrock is stirring.

V

The earliest known Native Americans of southwest Wisconsin, referred to by archaeologists as Paleo-Americans, lived at the edges of the great glaciers twelve thousand years ago. Later, Woodland Period

Native Americans built burial mounds in the hills above the Mississippi from 500 BC to 1,200 AD. The Mesquakie (and their cousins, the Sauk) were recent arrivals in the 1700s when the Iroquois drove them from their ancestral home near the Great Lakes.

By the 1820s, lead mining and promising farmland had brought European-Americans. In 1830 the U. S. government forced the Mesquakie and Sauk west of the Mississippi. Lead-miner George Wallace Jones acquired Sinsinawa Mound from the federal government and traded with the Mesquakie on the future Iowa shore.

A band of Sauk revolted against the expulsion and followed the warrior Black Hawk through western Illinois and Wisconsin in the Black Hawk War. Jones built a small military fort at Sinsinawa in1832 for local protection in case the hostilities erupted nearby. The structure still stands at the entrance to the Dominican complex, a relict of war and violent expulsion in a center dedicated to peace and justice.

Jones himself had a bigger career in mind. He became the first territorial representative in Washington, DC, for the Territory of Wisconsin and later moved across the river and became one of the first U.S. Senators for the new state of Iowa. He sold his Sinsinawa land in 1844 to an energetic, young Dominican missionary priest he had befriended, named Father Samuel Mazzuchelli.

VI

> There was no need of Italian marble for a
> pavement: that was found ready-made of
> the green grass in summer and hard
> frozen earth in winter.
> —Fr. Samuel Mazzuchelli, O.P.,
> regarding an Indian open-air
> tent church

If the first great spirit of Manitoumie gathered over the laying down of bedrock and the separation of waters, and the second great spirit arrived with the Native Americans, Sinsinawa Mound was en-spirited yet a third time with the arrival of Father Samuel Mazzuchelli, Order of Preachers. Within a few short years he would establish a men's college, then a Dominican motherhouse at the base of the Mound.

Sinsinawa was not even on Mazzuchelli's horizon yet in 1823, when, at the age of 17, he left his comfortable home in Milan, Italy, entered the Order of Preachers (commonly known as the Dominicans), and shortly thereafter responded to a call for missionaries to America. Mazzuchelli's first assignment after ordination in 1830 was to a wilderness ranging from Michigan's Macinac Island to Wisconsin's Green Bay, a region covering 52,500 square miles.

Mazzuchelli was missionary to the Menominee, Winnebago, Chippewa, and Ottawa in the area. In respect for the culture, language, and spirituality of the Native Americans—rare among missionaries of that era—Mazzuchelli's schools employed native teachers, respected native tongues, and allowed native students to live with their families instead of removing them to dormitories. With the help of interpreters, Mazzuchelli printed a book of Christian prayers in the Winnebago language. His Mackinac congregations "chanted psalms alternately in Latin and Chippewa," writes biographer Mary Cabrini Durkin. Mazzuchelli, she says, "recognized their Great Spirit as the God he served."

Of course, Mazzuchelli wasn't entirely immune to the prejudices of his time. His journal speaks of the native religion as an "imperfect idea of the divinity" and celebrates those natives who, while keeping some of their more "innocent" customs, nonetheless "reject every practice not comformable to the truth and sanctity of the Christian faith, which alone enables them to improve and civilize themselves." But when the white man's westward push robbed Native Americans of their homeland, Mazzuchelli came to their defense. He wrote to the Wisconsin Territorial Delegate to Congress, George Wallace Jones: "Most of our Indian wars are the natural and unavoidable consequence of the misconduct of the whites. Most of our Indian treaties are badly planned, unfairly ratified, and shamefully executed." In a letter to President Andrew Jackson, Mazzuchelli objected to the Indian Removal Act of 1830: "Before you encourage a new treaty . . . see whether the conditions of the old ones have been fulfilled."

By 1835 the Native American population had been forcibly removed from the Mackinac and Green Bay areas, and Mazzuchelli's missionary calling brought him several hundred miles south to the lands bounded by present-day Galena, Illinois, Dubuque, Iowa, and southwest Wisconsin. Here, recently immigrated Catholic Irishmen were working the lead-mines and immigrant Catholic Germans were plowing the prairie.

Mazzuchelli immediately went to work building twenty-five churches and chapels in the immigrant communities, many of them brick and limestone treasures that still exist. He was often architect and engineer for the churches he envisioned, yet he added his own manual sweat alongside that of the local parishioner-laborers. The Irish immigrants were so enamored of this hardworking Italian that they morphed his name to something more of their own, calling him "Father Matthew Kelly."

His empathy for hard laborers was evident already in his Mackinac days, when he wrote in his journal, "Those who held lower positions in the fur trade led a most laborious life in the wild country . . . while those who employed them were enjoying the delicacies and luxuries of the populous cities of the great republic."

Eventually, hard work and illness wore down the young priest, and in 1843 he was persuaded to return home to Italy to recuperate. In his convalescence he wrote a memoir of his missionary days and raised funds for missionary work. He didn't stay home long. By 1844 he was ready to return to Midwestern America, this time with the charge of developing a Dominican center in the southwest Wisconsin lands he had previously served as missionary.

Mazzuchelli founded Sinsinawa Mound College for men in 1846. But the men's college was short-lived, and by 1847, Mazzuchelli shifted the focus of Sinsinawa to women by inviting Dominican sisters to found a motherhouse at the Mound. From the start, Mazzuchelli gave women strong leadership roles. In his own family background, Mazzuchelli's mother had been co-owner of the family property; thus Mazzuchelli had no qualm about making the Mound's first four sisters the trustees of Sinsinawa, a rare occurrence at that time.

In 1852 he sold off Sinsinawa and moved the Dominican center to nearby Benton, Wisconsin. In 1854 he established St. Clara Academy for Women in Benton, teaching scripture, foreign language, music, physics, and astronomy, making use of his own telescope equipment.

But after Mazzuchelli's death in 1864, the sisters re-purchased

Sinsinawa and moved the school and motherhouse back to the
Mound. The academy expanded into a women's college, awarding its
first degrees in 1901, although the women's college moved in 1922
and the girls' academy closed in 1970.

Today, two hundred Dominican sisters live at Sinsinawa, many
of them retired but many still in active duty. The six hundred
Sinsinawa Dominican sisters across the country and abroad are
active as elementary, secondary, and college teachers, social workers,
therapists, physicians and nurses, HIV/AIDS ministers, counselors,
artists, carpenters, parish ministers, chaplains, and rural outreach
coordinators. The former residential girls academy now houses senior
citizens apartments. The complex includes a nursing home, historical
archives, bookstore, bread shop, community theater, Mazzuchelli
exhibit, and farm. Recent public retreats have included Women of the
Bible ("Bad Girls"), Yoga for Stress Relief, Contemplating the Psalms,
and Paint/Write Your Own Icon. The modernistic, circular Queen of
the Rosary Chapel is the soul of the complex, brightened with thirty-
seven diamond and triangular windows using the sun as a thematic
motif: "the sun as joy—incarnation; the sun as sorrow—redemption;
sun as glory—Pentecost eternal." Thirty-two thousand guests visit
Sinsinawa Mound every year.

Even with all this activity, Sinsinawa Mound remains a quiet
place, reflecting the Dominican mission of community, prayer, study,
and ministry.

But it is the earthen mound rising above the complex where the
real quiet exists, disturbed only by the wind.

VII

The land itself is sacred. But just like water seeps, flows, and gathers, the spirit, too, seems to favor certain glens, ridges, and passes,
and not always those which are most spectacular.

What I want to know is this: Did Mazzuchelli sense the spirit in
Manitoumie?

It's hard to say for sure from Mazzuchelli's journals whether he
loved nature. I think sometimes that among European-Americans a
love for nature is largely a modern sentiment—both a luxury in a

society largely sheltered from nature's cruelty, and a necessity in a world otherwise bent on destroying the environment. The pioneer, on the other hand, sometimes neither loved nor despised the natural world, but was simply *in* it—in it up to his boots and work sleeves.

The journals reveal Mazzuchelli living in the thick of nature. In Mackinac, he covers his 52,500 square-mile domain on horseback:

> The many swamps frequently constituted a serious obstacle, because one had to cross them on foot in order to lighten the horse. Often, in spite of all possible precautions, the noble beast broke through the thin crust covering the soft watery ground underneath. When such a misfortune occurred, it was not easy to get the animal on his feet, for his very effort to rise only sank him more deeply into the swamp and sometimes he was lost.

In winter, a horse-drawn sled gets him about the northland:

> In the cold season the beautiful and vast natural prairies of Wisconsin often provide the traveler an easy and convenient route over the snow which for several months covers them with its white mantle. . . . It is not easy to give a clear idea of a four hundred and twenty mile journey all alone, across a region still uncultivated, during a severe winter, in a sledge drawn by a single horse, crossing prairies, woods, rivers, and frozen lakes. . . . The inexperienced traveler must overcome many difficulties: there are unbridged streams with high banks, whose waters, fed by nearby springs, do not freeze; the ice is not always solid on the lakes and is very treacherous on certain rivers; in the hollows of the undulating prairies the snow is often heaped up by the winds in drifts of six or seven feet.

In his later home in Southwest Wisconsin, he contends with the Mississippi River en route to visiting a sick man:

He [Mazzuchelli writes of himself in the third person] found

that the ice no longer formed a solid bridge, but, broken up
by the warm temperature and the winds, was carried along
by the current. . . . The priest, with four lay persons, found no
means of crossing other than a narrow boat made from a tree
trunk which had been left on the river bank all winter. They
put it into the water and embarked without noticing that the
old boat had several cracks along the sides. When they were
nearly halfway across the river, the water began to pour in;
one of the passengers was pale and trembling with fright. The
steersman, however, a skillful man, courageously managed
the frail boat, ordering those who were seated not to move,
'Or else,' he said, 'we are lost.' Only the priest remained kneel-
ing and paddling with a single oar, while the steersman gave
orders to row faster.

But still Mazzuchelli evokes a certain awe in his encounters with
nature. As he embarks from Europe en route to America, he faces the
ocean breeze:

The Missionary enjoyed the awesome sight of the ocean when,
unchained and tempestuous, it seemed bent on destroying any
man who defied its anger. Clinging to the mainmast, he could
see the violent imperious waves venting their wrath upon the
ship, often as if trying to engulf it, flooding the entire deck
with their crests.

And, many years later, when an exhausted Mazzuchelli has finally
been convinced to temporarily return to his native Milan for rest, his
autobiography relates his homeward journey as he sets forth onto the
Mississippi:

The Missionary departed from the little city of Galena in a
steamboat to go down the majestic Mississippi. Four days later
he found the deepest delight in contemplating the visible
works of the Creator. . . . The rapid motion of the boat,
accelerated by the current, made the view of the hills, the

valleys, the meadows, woods, vast solitudes, numerous islands, and, at intervals, the new towns, pass before the eyes,
quickly change, and lose themselves in the distance. . . . When
nature is ready to put on her green mantle, she inspires that
sudden exclamation from the prophet David: 'Praise him, O
mountains and all ye hills; fruitful trees and all cedars' [Ps.
148:9]. The magnificent starry vault of the sky could alone
give an idea of the glorious eternity according to the words of
the same prophet: 'The heavens declare the glory of God, and
firmament proclaims his handiwork' [Ps. 19:1]. To the traveler
going swiftly down the river, while everything recedes, the sky
alone seems of the splendor, the glory, and the changelessness
of Paradise.

VIII

November 1. All Saints Day. The air is crisp, hinting at winter, the
sky a clear, pale blue. The air is light. It is 25 degrees outside, following an unusually cold October.

Shrines to the saints guard the edge of the woods. The shrine of
St. Dominic proclaims his birth in 1170. A cement-cast dog with a
cement-cast bone rests at his feet. Nearby is Our Lady of Lourdes
Grotto with an Italian-marble Madonna poised on native Niagara
limestone. Down the lane lies the sisters' cemetery, the uniform headstones glistening white in the sun.

At the end of the lane lies the "labyrinth," a circular, brick pathway that winds and weaves inward toward a central focal point, then
unweaves itself back to the periphery, twisting and wending, drawing
you into its center and pushing you away again. Walking the labyrinth reenacts the spiritual journey. Dr. Lauren Artress, designer of
the Sinsinawa Labyrinth completed in 1999, writes, "It helps [people]
see their lives in the context of a path, a pilgrimage. They realize that
they are not human beings on a spiritual path but spiritual beings on
a human path." The labyrinth, with its thought-deflecting, repetitive
footpath of 6,000 bricks, echoes the "rosary, Buddhist walking
meditation, indigenous walk-abouts, the way of the cross."

I begin walking the labyrinth, trying to unthink my mind, but

thoughts keep cluttering back. In the cold cross-winds, I watch my
feet, step after step, not knowing where I'm at in the big circle. Time
after time I think I've reached the center, until the labyrinth turns
me outward again. Finally, after treading the four quarter-paths, I
arrive at the center, and look up, at last, from my feet. The sun slices
through the barren trees, dazzling and hurting my eyes.

In the center, dead oak leaves litter the ground. I imagine the
labyrinth deep in winter, snow blotting out the path, and the bricks
re-emerging in spring snow-melt. I listen to the wind, and suddenly,
finally, that which I've searched for—nothing. The emptiness of
thought. Thought gone blank.

My sore back returns me to the thinking world. It is, once again,
All Saints Day, and wind-strewn. Leaves twirl and rake like snow
flurries. The next stop is the restored oak savanna, home to twenty
different species of flowering plants and grasses, now tangled and
brown with first frosts. The oak savanna is this region's most preva-
lent natural flora, combining lush prairie grasslands with the shade
of small, scattered groves of burr oak. Native prairie required fire to
burn away encroaching trees. But burr oaks grow a hardy bark, re-
sistant to fire, and so the oak savanna was dotted with these majestic
trees and their craggy, horizontal limbs.

The pilgrimage now leads up into the woods. Here, the forest
floor is strewn with maple leaves. A tree branch grunts and moans
in the wind. A leaf falls on my head, covering me like a hat. The big
slanted rock slab, which I had found in September, is now covered in
leaves. The wind sounds like ocean surf.

The path winds upward through the woods and then emerges
from the forest at the clearing at the top of Sinsinawa Mound. The
sun slices through, brilliant and warm on my shoulders and face. Two
deer crash through the woods, white tails flickering like flame. The
thinning woods reveal the outline of the Sinsinawa buildings. All
Saints Day and the beginning of November—riding time like boats
on an urgent river. It is time, now, to move to shelter. Winter will
soon come blustering in.

But decay has its beauty, too. Back down again at the base of the Mound, a dead tree's polished root, barkless and brilliant with flowing whorls, has snaked about Madonna's feet.

IX

For many years, Sinsinawa Mound was home to the Churches' Center for Land and People (CCLP). Sisiter Miriam Brown, O.P., who directed CCLP from its 1989 inception until July 2003, cites its dual mission to keep the churches involved with and informed on rural issues and to "put out there our own ethics and values" regarding the family farm. CCLP regards issues such as biotech and corporate farming from ethical, spiritual, and earth stewardship frameworks.

The Dominicans likewise farmed several hundred acres at the base of the Mound until 2004. In the early years, sisters themselves tilled the land. In recent years, a full-time farm manager ran the farm and dairy herd, adhering to Sustainable Agriculture goals of soil conservation, minimizing chemical treatments, and reducing fuel costs. When the farm manager left in March 2004, the sisters made the difficult decision to sell the dairy herd and rent the land to neighboring farmers. But they still insisted on Sustainable Agriculture practices.

"We always had the farm from the beginning, have always taken seriously the caring of the earth. Through that farm we identify with others' problems and concerns for the land and identify with the struggle of our neighbors," says Brown. "Father Mazzuchelli was very aware of the living conditions of people in his time. He spoke out on public issues, like the Civil War, brother killing brother. There has always been a strong sense of social justice in our colleges and schools."

The Sinsinawa Dominicans have issued a land vision statement of their own:

"The following Judeo-Christian principles shape our relationship to our Sinsinawa land:
- The earth belongs to God;
- We have a special responsibility to care for all creation;
- The land is given as a gift to all humankind and is

meant to benefit both present and future generations;
- In working with the land, we are 'co-creators with
  God, guiding the land's productive power and
  conserving the land's natural gifts.'"

Holy land. Sacred place.
Manitoumie.

X

All ground is hallowed. It is earth-mother, giving sustenance. We
build upon her, plow her fields, eat her fruits. Without these, we do
not live. When we do these things injudiciously, we destroy her.

All ground is hallowed, but do some grounds harbor a special
spirit?

Sinsinawa Mound rises impressively above the general plateau
above the Mississippi Valley. It is, I have said, a landmark in every
direction. Even so, it does not soar like the Rocky Mountains or wrap
winds about itself like the Himalayas.

The Great Spirit has chosen it for reasons unrevealed.

XI

Late Winter.

From a distance, the bare tree branches make the Mound look
brown in the relentless winter cold. But up close, the ground is
whitened from a light two-inch snowfall the night before. With the
temperature warming today, though, the snow lies wet and heavy.
It is a good "packing" snow, as we used to call it as kids, and I wad
a few snowballs and hurl them at tree trunks. They hit home with a
luscious splat—white and sloppy pockmarks on the bark.

Hiking today, I've played cat-and-mouse with a woman in the
woods. I see her footprints on the path ahead of me, and where they
veer off, I veer, too, wondering what she is pursuing. Around a bend I
finally see her moving amid the trees, and I change my direction so as
not to disturb her. She is seeking her own solitude, and I mine.

I keep my eyes open for . . . something. Above me, an owl graces the sky in a swift arc. Beside me, the moss on the backs of boulders is white with thick frost. Winter birds are scattered among the top branches in the forest, and in the distance, the ongoing chatter of cawing.

The woman appears again, thirty-ish, dressed in black winter coat and slacks, rolling a large matted snowball along the path. I veer off again, and when I pass this way later I find a snowman along the path. He is short, as last night's snowfall wasn't deep, built with the required twigs for arms, but sporting a full face, with a triangular mouth shaped from bent reeds.

The warming continues. It won't be long before the oaks and maples leaf out again, until the forest undergrowth creeps and stirs, and, in the general thaw, perhaps a great boulder will heave, split, and tumble this year. On the way home I stop near a backwaters of the Mississippi, and as I exit my car, a honking V-formation of geese is taking flight just overhead and headed, resolutely, north.

And out on the water on this grey day, the ice is mottled, breaking up after last week's freeze. Just below the bridge pilings, a triangle of winter-black water is exposed.

XII

I have to work to be aware of any spirits at all some days. Life, work, and family have plenty of legitimate needs clamoring for my attention.

Some days I can quell all the squabble in my mind just long enough to be aware of my own spirit, my own thoughts, my own sensory intake, my own sense of being in the present moment. And then the cares, responsibilities, and distractions of everyday life crowd in again.

But when it's good—when it's really, really good—there are plenty of spirits here, whipped in the wind, sighing in the tree branches, and burgeoning from the mossy boulders heaved up from the bedrock.

For the Great Spirit dwells here.

Manitoumie.

Where the Earth Breathes:
A Vow of Stability

Still, the profound change
has come upon them: rooted, they
grip down and begin to awaken
—William Carlos Williams, "Spring and All"

I am gazing out my office window. I have a fifth-floor office in a century-old building at Loras College, on a bluff facing east. Before and beneath me lie the streets of Dubuque, Iowa, dusted last night with a fresh four-inch snowfall. Steep hills descend to the river valley nested with Victorian homes, church steeples, and an eclectic clutter of nineteenth-century downtown facades. A bit further lies a frozen stretch of Mississippi River, the U.S. 151 bridge crawling with steady but not crowded traffic, a slow-moving train on the opposite shore, and steep-sided Wisconsin bluffs in a wintry mosaic of brown and white. The view is, in short, a fine diversion from grading papers.

This place is home.

Having said that, I've left the word "this" intentionally vague. By home, I could be referring to Loras College, where I have taught for more than twenty-five years. I could be referring to the 1906-constructed house where I live and where we still ponder whether the limestone-walled basement corner room may have been a summer kitchen or a horse barn. I could be referring to Dubuque, which has been my home for fifty years, and my family's since the 1880s. I could be referring to the Driftless Land, to North America, or to the world. For all of these are my home.

But in another sense, I can't know or care for the world without first knowing and caring for my local home, without first developing a sense of place.

And how is any of that that the slightest bit meaningful to my students, who have come from other places and will graduate and move again? Or to my children, who love the faraway mountains more than the river, and who, like most Americans, will move, on average, every seven years and change careers just as often? To a culture in which one city looks like another with its replicated box-store giants, or which finds its strongest allegiances to virtual, electronic communities? Have I, at mid-life, simply settled into anachronistic beliefs?

After reading Scott Russell Sanders' *Staying Put: Making a Home in a Restless World* with my Nonfiction Writing class, I asked my students to write briefly about the ways in which they are "wanderers" and the ways in which they are "rooted." There was, of course, a tug and pull between these two. The same students who "want to see the world" and "have new experiences" are simultaneously "rooted" in family and faith, for example. It is healthy to be both rooted and wanderer.

Sanders reminded us, as we traveled through his essays, that although American culture did not invent "wandering," we certainly have perfected it. Native Americans found their way to the Americas more than twelve thousand years ago across icy lands of the Bering Strait made passable by the retreat of the oceans during the last Ice Age. They dispersed across North, Central, and South America. The climate warmed, the ice retreated, and the oceans rebounded. Soon enough the wanderers were cut off from their Asian origins. The rest of our ancestors, of course, arrived at various times within the last four hundred years, coming to the Americas for gold, for land, for jobs, for religious freedom, as punishment, to escape starvation, as draft evaders, or were transported against their will as slaves.

Nothing new in that civics lesson, except that we haven't stopped moving ever since: westward expansion, plowing the plains, the Underground Railroad, and California migration, where, as Joan Didion writes, we'd better get it right because we've run out of continent. Now the migration is to the South, where Americans take refuge from the (ironically ever-milder) Northern winters.

But wandering, as Sanders points out, is pretty much a human genetic trait, along with speaking and storytelling, a trait that signifies what it means to be human. The peoples of the "old world" of Europe and Asia wandered to their present locations out of Africa, and even indigenous peoples are often nomadic. We learn to scope out the neighborhood and wonder what lies over the mountain. And much good has come from our human wanderings: the enrichment of cultures and literatures, the spread and expansion of knowledge and trade, the sharing of foods and agricultural practices.

Of course, the modern world has brought wandering to new heights, with the automobile, jet, internet, and a sense of ourselves in a "virtual world" that is often not rooted in physical locale at all.

But there is a downside to our wandering, and, especially, to our loss of the sense of place. Sanders notes that "many of the worst abuses—of land, forests, animals, and communities—have been carried out by [people who have ceased to root themselves in a sense of place.]" A century ago, speculators enticed pioneers to break the high-plains prairie sod, not understanding that prairie grasses held the soil intact in an arid land, and the 1930s Dust Bowl ensued. But even those of us not on the move may lose our connection to and understanding of the land. In my home state of Iowa, we have plowed or paved nearly every available acre. Iowa rates nearly last in the country for the amount of land set aside for parks and wildlife refuges. Agricultural and commercial water-runoff courses through the state's streams, bowls into the Mississippi River, and feeds a Dead Zone in the Gulf of Mexico where nothing grows or lives for hundreds of miles past the great river's mouth.

These things happen when we lose touch with the land, resist rooting down in the place where we live, or fail to understand how our place connects inch by inch, acre by acre, to the next place, and to the whole ecosystem of earth.

———————————

Since 1849, Trappist monks have lived at New Melleray Abbey, fifteen miles west of my home in Dubuque, deeply connected to their own corner of the prairie. They were invited here by Dubuque's first Catholic Bishop, Matthias Loras, from their home at Mount Melleray Abbey in Ireland, where, like the rest of their countrymen, they were starving through the potato famine. About thirty monks still live at New Melleray, many of them aged. Many have lived their entire adult lives at the abbey, their vows dating as far back as 1942, although a handful of monks have taken vows in the past ten years.

There are many kinds of monks, St. Benedict reminds his readers in the opening to his sixth century Rule for monastics. Among others, there are hermits, like the Desert Fathers, the earliest Christian monks who favored the caves of the Egyptian desert. There are wandering monks, "who keep going their whole life long from one province to another, staying three or four days at a time in different cells as guests. Always roving and never settled." But Benedict writes for the Cenobites, those who live in community and who vow, among other things, a life of "stability." They will remain, the rest of their lives forward, at this abbey alone, and will likewise be buried within.

At New Melleray Abbey, rows of simple iron crosses in an interior courtyard mark the graves of the monks, who are buried in simplicity, with no casket, just a thin shroud separating them, for a while, from the soil.

The vow of stability, for monks, means a pledge to remain at the abbey, to persevere in the liturgies of the day, to work humbly, to own nothing, and to regard the tools, implements, and vessels of the abbey as sacred. Inevitably, this attachment to the abbey translates into a deep connection to the land on which it sits. Thomas Merton, a twentieth century Trappist from Gethsemane Abbey in Kentucky, explains: "How necessary it is for monks to work in the fields, in the rain, in the sun, in the mud, in the clay, in the wind: these are our spiritual directors and our novice-masters. They form our contemplation. They instill us with virtue. They make us as stable as the land we live in."

Stability for the rest of us does not mean—should not mean and cannot mean—vowing to stay put in the same locale where we've been born or landed our first job. We do live in the real world, where mobility is the rule of life. But stability is a call to be in the fields, in the rain, the mud, and the clay no matter where we're at, no matter for how long. Our dirty hands, wet faces and backs, and sore feet are testimony to our contact and connectedness to the earth that birthed us and will receive us back again.

I light out on a winter's hike toward the preserve near my house. Today it's hard going, though. Repeated cycles of ice and snow and thaws have left the wooded bottomland with a thick and icy crust that I sink into about every third step.

It's a long way back into the woods to where I'd intended to go, past 50-foot rock outcroppings and 100-foot bluffs, past century-old lead-mine pits, past a limestone tower formation called the Twin Sisters, past the railroad tracks, past an overlook of the Catfish Creek valley. Can't say I'm up to crunching through the ice crust all the way back to the far reaches of the preserve, so I decide instead to use the crusty snow to my advantage and climb a steeply wooded hillside, using a hiking stick and digging the edges of my boots down into the snow.

I've been up through these woods and on the top-land clearing before, but not for a couple of years. The lead-mine pits are more numerous up here. A scraggly woods has grown in around them in the 150 years since they were last mined, but here and there a burr oak with great lateral branches attests that these hills were once savannas thinly forested with the massive trees that had leisurely spread their branches above the prairie.

The lead-mine pits are, for the most part, easy to spot. They dot the upper third of the hillside (although there are others in the bottom lands as well) with deep circular scoops and tell-tale rock-strewn edges. Most stretch about six feet across, although they can be as wide as twenty. In some cases they were the entry points to lead-mine shafts, but the older pits merely scratched along a surface vein, so it's not uncommon to find four or five in a row—usually east to west—where someone had scored a hit along a backbone.

If this were Ireland—and these miners *were* Irish immigrants, by and large—and if my ancestors had come upon these rounded pits with no prior knowledge of their making, no doubt we'd attribute them to fairies.

Sometimes, however, in a rocky terrain like this it is hard to tell which is lead mine and which is cave. I find the latter at an indentation in the hill I'd spied on my climb up. Instead of a shallow scooped out pit, I find a vertical shaft walled with bedrock limestone sinking away beneath the forest floor. The mouth of the cave is about twice my girth and ominously ringed with sloping ice. My stomach crawls at the mere thought of what a slip could do, as there would be no way to climb back out and—judging by the lack of footprints in the snow—one ought not to count on a passerby. Curiosity doesn't even tempt this cat, except to find a stone to toss inside, to hear how long it takes to clatter to the cave floor. It takes . . . long enough.

Switching tactics, I grab a handful of powdery snow and sprinkle it above the opening, and the light puff of warm air escaping from the depths scatters the powder as if it were confetti.

This yawning of the earth intrigues me! I could tell you about the consistency of cave temperatures, cool against summer air and warm against the winter, could tell you how the warmer air will rise out of a vertical shaft in winter. But if it's all the same to you, I must tell you instead that the earth itself is breathing, and its mouth—one of many I am sure—is located on a hillside near my home.

You will find it if you venture out across the snow in the Driftless Land, if you know which valley to enter and which hillside to climb, if you can locate the vertical cave shaft in the overgrown woods.

I won't guarantee that I will find it back when I go there next. I'm notoriously bad with directions. Or maybe, like fairy rings in Ireland, it will simply pick up and move.

But for a moment, I was in contact with the bedrock of my home. I felt its breath.

Along with the bleak stories of those who have abused the land are the stories of connection, of those who have learned the Benedictine quality of stability, of those who have rooted down in a particular place for the while they are here. A professor I know brings his students to the Mines of Spain to collect prairie seed for new plantings. Citizens in Dubuque fight to save the river bluffs from overdevelopment. A wildlife refuge is procured by the County Conservation Board. Students and their teachers haul away brushy trees and restore an oak savanna.

The world is spiritual, the world is physical. The world is rain and sun and mud and clay. Henry David Thoreau nearly trips over himself in *The Maine Woods* regarding its tactile marvels: "Talk of mysteries—Think of our life in nature—daily to be shown matter, to come in contact with it—rocks, trees, wind on our cheeks! the solid earth! the actual world! the common sense! Contact! Contact!" Then turns inward, as if pondering the gaping hole in the ground: "Who are we? where are we?"

Scott Russell Sanders likewise ponders the internal tug of the external world: "It has taken me half a lifetime of searching to realize that the likeliest path to the ultimate ground leads through my local ground. I mean the land itself, with its creeks and rivers, its weather, seasons, stone outcroppings, and all the plants and animals that share it. I cannot have a spiritual center without having a geographical one."

Thomas Merton, Trappist monk, vows his stability to the forest: "The silence of the forest is my bride and the sweet dark warmth of the whole world is my love and out of the heart of the dark warmth comes the secret that is heard only in silence, but it is the root of all the secrets that are whispered by all the lovers in their beds all over the world."

My college students will be graduating in a few weeks. One will go off to study in Ireland. Several are returning home to Chicago. Their flight patterns from past years have been varied, landing them for work or study in Seattle and Denver, Texas and Michigan, and Washington, DC. One of my former students taught in the Peace Corps in Eastern Europe, wrote for a computer magazine in Egypt, and then found himself back in the states in Milwaukee and then Rochester, working for non-profit organizations.

The vow of stability does not mean living life in one place, going back to one's hometown and staying there forever. In fact, rooting down and connecting to place is more of a frame of mind than a matter of time lived in a single locale. Some people, like me, *have* lived most of their lives in one town, but you can root down just as certainly when you move from place to place.

I am invited to speak to a small gathering of graduating seniors. When you move to a new place, I tell them, look around. Find out what brought the people here, learn how the land was formed. Understand what grows here, and why, and what creatures live here, and *have lived* here before. Pause and think before you turn a spade of ground, whether for a new house, a new shopping center, or a new shed in the backyard. That is not to say *don't build* that house, supermarket, or shed. But *pause and think* before you begin: Is this what is best for this place, not just now, but for the long run? Sometimes the answer will be yes, sometimes it will be no. But it is important to ask the question.

I tell them, I don't know how much you have explored *this* place that is right now still your home in the Driftless Land. At the Mines of Spain south of town, the area's first lead-miners scraped out small conical ore pits, and today the weathered indentations lie silent and recaptured in the woods. Go there, find them. Near the Little Maquoketa River north of town, a brisk hike up more than one hundred railroad-tie steps will bring you face to face with the Native American past in the form of burial mounds. Go *there*. At Swiss Valley you will find rock outcroppings that puncture the soil like the great bone of earth piercing through skin. Here and there are prairie remnants. And even if you've rarely left campus, surely you've seen, across the river, that mound on the horizon, Sinsinawa, but did you know that it was holy ground, not just to the Dominicans who have called it home for 150 years, but to the Native Americans before them, who called the region "Manitoumie," Where the Great Spirit Dwells? Go there, too.

———————————

The monks take their vow of stability.

How well they must know, over time, the sounds their footsteps make in the cloister, the smells of food in the refectory, the slant of light in the chapel at Vespers. The tactile physicality is the contact point leading inward to the spirit, much like the corpus Christi leads to the eternal.

You and I may live in a different world than the monks. But a vow of stability—of looking and seeing and touching that which is right here before us—may help us find that place in the hillside where the earth opens its mouth and breathes.

DRIFTLESS

That ice flows like slow-motion liquid
might be news to some,
inscribed as it is in drumlins
and moraines the ancient
glaciers left behind.

Slowly, repeatedly, the glaciers awakened
and crept down from the north,
scoured the plains,
and slid
around, beside, behind
the Driftless Land.

An island in a sea
of creeping floes,
a rugged boat
with rocky masts
that prick the ice pack,
adrift
in some polar vertigo.

But it is the ice that floats,
not you,
secured to bedrock
in the Driftless Land.

SOURCES

"Introduction: The Driftless Land"
Prior, Jean C. *Landforms of Iowa.* Iowa City: U of Iowa P, 1991.
United States Fish and Wildlife Service. "Driftless Area National
    Wildlife Refuge." http://www.fws.gov/midwest/driftless/.
United States Fish and Wildlife Service. "Driftless Area National
    Wildlife Refuge: Comprehensive Conservation Plan," 2006.

"The Rivers That Bring Us Together"
Auge, Thomas, Ph.D. "Destruction of a Culture." *Gateway Heritage.*
    (Fall 1980): 32-45.
Effigy Mounds Historic Resource Study. Prepared for National Park
    Service. http://www.nps.gov/efmo/web/hrs/hrst.htm. , Aug. 2003.
Lenzendorf, Dennis. *Effigy Mounds: A Guide to Effigy Mounds
    National Monument.* Fort Washington, PA: Eastern National
    Press, 2000.
Lenzendorf, Dennis. Interview and Guided Tour, 4 December 2004.
Marquette, Jacques, SJ. *Voyages of Marquette.* Reprinted in French/
    English text, Ann Arbor, MI: University microfilms, Inc.
Wilkie, William, Ph.D. *Dubuque on the Mississippi: 1788-1988.*
    Dubuque, IA: Loras College Press, 1987.

"Winter Here"
Ehrlich, Gretel. *The Solace of Open Spaces.* New York: Penguin Books,
    1985.
Norris, Kathleen. *Dakota: A Spiritual Geography.* Boston: Houghton-
    Mifflin, 1993.

"Ice Age!"
"Antarctic Ice Shelf Collapse Blamed on Warming Climate."
    Environmental News Service. 26 March 2008. http://www.ens-
    newswire.com/ens/mar2008/2008-03-26-01.asp.
Boyle, Alan. "Greenland's glaciers losing ice at faster rate." *MSNBC.*
    16 February 2006. http://www.msnbc.msn.com/id/11385475/.

Crawford, Dave. "The Geology of Interstate Park." A Minnesota
    Department of Natural Resources publication.
Dillard, Annie. *Teaching a Stone to Talk*. New York: HarperPerennial,
    1982.
Dott, Robert H., Jr., and John W. Attig. *Roadside Geology of Wiscon-
    sin*. Missoula, MT: Mountain Press, 2004.
Ehrlich, Gretel. *The Future of Ice*. New York: Pantheon Books, 2004.
Gont, Rod. Naturalist, Chippewa Moraine Ice Age State Recreation
    Area, New Auburn, Wisconsin. Interview and guided tour, 7 April
    2008.
Gore, Al. *An Inconvenient Truth*. New York: Rodale, 2006.
Ice Age Park and Trail Foundation. http://www.iceagetrail.org/.
    9 May 2008.
Musolf, Gene, et al. "Glacial Geology: Ice On the Land." http://www.
    iceagetrail.org/PDF/GlacialGeology_Musolf.pdf. January 2005.
Prior, Jean C. *Landforms of Iowa*. Iowa City: U of Iowa P, 1991.
Tassier-Surine, Stephanie. Research Geologist, Iowa Geological
    Survey. Correspondence, February 2008.

"Sacred Place: The Landscape of Memory"
Brueggemann, Walter. *The Land: Place as Gift, Promise, and Chal-
    lenge in Biblical Faith*. Philadelphia, PA: Fortress, 1977.
Chittister, Joan, OSB. *Wisdom Distilled From the Daily: Living the
    Rule of St. Benedict Today*. San Francisco: HarperSanFrancisco,
    1990.
Lane, Beldon C. *Landscapes of the Sacred: Geography and Narrative in
    American Spirituality*. Mahwah, NJ: Paulist Press, 1988.
Sheldrake, Philip. *Spaces for the Sacred: Place, Memory, and Identity*.
    Baltimore, MD: The Johns Hopkins U P, 2001.

"Chasing Black Hawk"
Black Hawk State Historic Site, Rock Island, IL. http://www.black-
    hawkpark.og/index.htm.
Black Sparrow Hawk. *Black Hawk: An Autobiography*. Ed. Donald
    Jackson. Original Publication: Cincinnati, 1833. Reprinted publi-
    cation, with notes and commentary: U of Illinois P, 1987.

Braun, Robert A. "Black Hawk's War: April 5–August 2, 1832—A Chronology." http://www.geocities.com/old_lead/bhwchron.htm. Sept. 2001.

"The Deep Snow." http://www.illinoishistory.com/deepsnow.htm. Reprinted from the January 28, 1968 issue of *The Illinois Intelligencer* as part of Illinois' Sesquicentennial Celebration.

"Indian Campaign of 1832." *Military and Naval Magazine of the United States.* 1 Aug. 1833: 321-333.

Lewis, James, Ph.D. "The Black Hawk War of 1832." 2000 Abraham Lincoln Historical Digitization Project. http://lincoln.lib.niu. edu/blackhawk/index.html.

Miller, Stanley. "Massacre At Bad Axe." *American History Illustrated.* April 1984: 30-35, 48.

Thwaites, Rueben Gold. *How George Rogers Clark Won the Northwest: And Other Essays in Western History.* Chicago: A.C. McClurg, 1903. Digitized.

Trask, Kerry A. *Black Hawk: The Battle for the Heart of America.* New York: Henry Holt, 2006.

Wisconsin Historical Society. "The Black Hawk War." http://www. wisconsinhistory.org/turningpoints/tp-012/?action=more_essay.

Wisconsin Historical Society. "Historic Diaries: Black Hawk War Documents." http://www.wisconsinhistory.org/diary/blackhawk-war.asp.

"Maquoketa Caves: The Landscape Beneath"
Karst Waters Institute. "What Is Karst and Why Is It Important?" http://www.karstwaters.org/kwitour/whatiskarst.htm.

"Maquoketa Caves State Park." http://www.stateparks.com/maquoketa_caves.html.

"Mississippi Refuge
Male, Clyde. Assistant District Manager, Upper Mississippi River National Wildlife and Fish Refuge, McGregor District. Interview 22 April 2008.

Stravers, Jon (Hawk). Audubon Society Raptor Inventory Special-
    ist. Interview 15 April, 2008. Guided boat tour and interview, 21
    April 2008.
United States Fish and Wildlife Service. "Upper Mississippi River
    National Wildlife & Fish Refuge." http://www.fws.gov/refuges/
    profiles/index.cfm?id=32579.

"Whitewater–Lost Canyon"
Gullett, Larry. Director, Jones County, Iowa, Conservation Board.
    Interview, 29 Jan. 2008.
Henneberry, Richard. Interview, 27 March 2008.
Lawler Ammon, Jenny. Naturalist, Dubuque County Conservation
    Board. Interview, 2 Feb. 2008.
Stone, Larry. "Iowa's Grand Canyon." *The Iowan.* May/June 2007: 26-
    30.
Walton, Robert. Retired Directory, Dubuque County, Iowa, Conser-
    vation Board. Interview and guided tour, 9 March 2007.

"Kickapoo Valley Reserve"
Hubbuch, Chris. "Soldiers Grove: Relocated town spared heavy flood
    damage; former site inundated." *La Crosse Tribune.* 22 June 2008.
    http://www.lacrossetribune.com/articles/2008/06/22/news/00lead.
    txt.
Kickapoo Valley Reserve. http://kvr.state.wi.us/. Accessed 13 May
    2008.
Kickapoo Valley Reserve Visitors Center. 8 April 2008.
Mississippi Valley Archaeological Center. "Western Wisconsin Rock
    Art Sites." http://www.uwlax.edu/mvac/SpecificSites/RockArt.
    htm. Accessed 12 May 2008.
West, Marcy. Executive Director, Kickapoo Valley Reserve. Telephone
    Interview, 7 May 2008.

"Savanna Army Depot"
"Base Re-Alignment and Closure." GlobalSecurity.Org. http://www.
    globalsecurity.org/military/facility/brac.htm. 27 Sept. 2004.

Division of Conservation Planning. "Lost Mound Unit, Upper Mississippi River National Wildlife and Fish Refuge Environmental Assessment." http://www.fws.gov/Midwest/planning/LostMound/index.html. 14 April 2008.

Erikson, Kurt. "Tiny Thomson Still Waiting for Prison to Pay Off." http://realcostofprisons.org/blog/archives/2007/12/il_tiny_thomson.html. 15 Dec. 2007.

"Fertilizer from thin air—new technologies improve an old idea." News Release. Northern Illinois University. http://www.niu.edu/PubAffairs/RELEASES/2008/july/N-Ovation%20Process.shtml. 8 July 2008.

Illinois Natural History Survey. "Lost Mound Field Station." Institute of Natural Resource Sustainability, University of Illinois at Urbana-Champaign, http://www.inhs.uiuc.edu/fieldstations/lost-mound/. July 2009.

Kunke, RuthAnne, Inga Olsen, and Ross E. Paulson. *80 Years of Service—Savanna Ordnance Depot: In the Defense of Our Nation*. Rock Island, IL: Augustana College, 1996.

"Lost Mound National Wildlife Refuge." An Illinois Department of Natural Resources & Upper Mississippi River National Wildlife and Fish Refuge publication.

"Lost Mound National Wildlife Refuge: Environmental Assessment." United States Fish and Wildlife Service. http://midwest.fws.gov/planning/lostmoundtop.htm. 8 Sept. 2003.

"NIU makes match that leads to $1 million grant." News Release. Northern Illinois University, http://www.niu.edu/PubAffairs/RELEASES/2008/july/N-ovation.shtml. 8 July 2008.

Reber, Craig. "Lost Mound Unit Makes Progress, Faces Challenges." *The Telegraph Herald*. 27 Aug. 2003.

U.S. Environmental Protection Agency. "Region 5 Superfund—Savanna Army Depot Activity." http://www.epa.gov/R5Super/npl/illinois/IL3210020803.htm. Accessed 4 April 2008.

I would like to thank the following persons for allowing me to interview them, tag along with them on their work, and return with follow-up questions:

- Marty Altensey: employee of Stickle Warehousing
- Beth Baranski: Baranski, Hammer, and Associates, and Lost Mound Action Team member
- Ed Britton: United States Fish & Wildlife Service
- John Clarke: BRAC Environmental Coordinator
- Harry Drucker: co-founder of Friends of the Depot
- Gary Frederick: President, Fluidic Micro-Controls and Vice President, N-Ovation.
- Warren Jackman: founder of Riverport Railroad
- Diane Komiskey: Executive Director of Jo-Carroll LRA
- Randy Nÿboer: Illinois Department of Natural Resources
- Jim Rachuy: Founder of Illinois Chapter of Prairie Enthusiasts
- John Rutherford: former member of the Jo-Carroll LRA
- Marty Sheehy: employee of Stickle Warehousing
- Rick Stickle: founder of Stickle Warehousing
- Bob Wehrle: former member of the Jo-Carroll LRA
- Dan Wenny: At the time of our field trip, Wenny was Associate Research Scientist for the Illinois Natural History Survey, a division of the University of Illinois at Urbana-Champaign.

"The Mountain That Soaks In the Water"

Bua, Deborah, and Margaret Truax. *Trempealeau Wisconsin, A Little History*. Trempealeau, WI: Trempealeau County Historical Society, 1978.

Lilla, Jennifer. Park Ranger, Trempealeau National Wildlife Refuge. Interview and guided tour, 13 Jan. 2006.

McMillin, Laurie Hovell. *Buried Indians: Digging Up the Past in a Midwestern Town*. Madison, WI: U of Wisconsin P, 2006.

"Prairie's Edge Wildlife Drive." Self-Guided Tour, Trempealeau National Wildlife Refuge. U.S. Government Printing Office, 1996.

Trempealeau National Wildlife Refuge. http://fws.gov/trempe-leau.10 June 2006.

"Manitoumie. Sinsinawa."
Durkin, Mary Carbrini, OSU, and Mary Nona McGreal, OP. *Always On Call: Samuel Mazzuchelli of the Order of Preachers.* Editions du Signe, 2000.
Gavlinger, Mary Ellen (O.P.) Dominican historian. Telephone interview, 3 Aug. 2004.
"The Labyrinth." Pamphlet, Sinsinawa Mound Center.
Lane, Beldon C. *Landscapes of the Sacred.* New York: Paulist Press, 1988.
Mazzuchelli, Samuel. *The Memoirs of Fr. Samuel Mazzuchelli, O.P.* tr. Sr. Maria Michele Armato, o.p., and Sr. Mary Jeremy Finnegan, o.p. Chicago: The Priory Press, 1967. (First published in Milan, Italy, 1844).
"Sinsinawa Mound." http://www.sinsinawa.org.
Various historical and geological sources consulted at Sinsinawa Mound Historical Archives.

Special thanks to the Dominican Sisters who taught me at St. Joseph's elementary school in Dubuque, Iowa, 1966-1973. I realize now how progressive and forward-thinking these sisters really were.

"Where the Earth Breathes: A Vow of Stability"

Merton, Thomas. The Sign of Jonas. Trappist, Kentucky : Abbey of Our Lady of Gethsemane, 1953.
————. *Dancing in the Water of Life.* New York: HarperCollins, 1997.
New Melleray Abbey. http://www.newmelleray.org/. Jan. 28, 2008.
Sanders, Scott Russell. *Staying Put: Making a Home In a Restless World.* Boston: Beacon P, 1993.
Thoreau, Henry David. *The Maine Woods.* New York: Viking P, 1985.